W9-CFI-066

Higher Learning

Higher Learning

Derek Bok

Harvard University Press
Cambridge, Massachusetts
and London, England
1986

Printed in the United States of America
10 9 8 7 6 5 4 3 2 1

This book is printed on acid-free paper, and its binding materials have been chosen for strength and durability.

Library of Congress Cataloging-in-Publication Data

Bok, Derek Curtis.
Higher learning.

Includes index.
1. Education, Higher—United States. 2. Universities and colleges—United States. 3. Professional education—United States. I. Title.
LA227.3.B63 1986 378.73 86-9876
ISBN 0-674-39175-6 (alk. paper)

To Sissela

Acknowledgments

Many friends helped me immeasurably by reading drafts of all or part of this book. Rather than specify the contributions made by each, let me simply express my great appreciation for the advice and criticism I have received from Burton Dreben, Henry Rosovsky, Roland Christensen, Dean Whitla, Burton Clark, and Graham Allison. Since my job makes it difficult to spend hours in the library, I have also benefited greatly from the able research assistance provided me by several people: William Neumann on undergraduate education and continuing education, George Baker III on professional education, and Barbara Graham, Joan Gulovsen, and Eileen Jay on the applications of technology to teaching. All of these provided me not only with research assistance but with the opportunity for much valuable discussion about the subjects on which they worked.

It would be impossible to express in words the thanks I owe to my loyal office colleagues, Julie Boruvka, Florence Gaylin, Elizabeth Keul, Priscilla Kinnear, and Marilyn Schmalenberger, for putting up with my endless drafts and redrafts. Above all, I am grateful to my wife, Sissela, who has read each chapter more than once and given me invaluable advice throughout.

Contents

Higher Learning

Introduction

When I began teaching at Harvard Law School more than a quarter of a century ago, I found much that exceeded my expectations. No group of students could have been more supportive or more patient with my early mistakes than the small venturesome band that chose to study Labor Law with me at nine o'clock on Friday and Saturday mornings. No colleagues could have been more welcoming than the same senior professors who had seemed so forbidding to me as a student only a few years before.

Amid these unexpected pleasures, I encountered only a single disappointment. One of my reasons for choosing to teach rather than practice law was the thought of mingling with scholars from a wide variety of fields. I had looked forward to spirited lunches at the Faculty Club with archaeologists fresh from digging in exotic lands and astronomers brimming with theories about life on other planets. Alas, nothing could have been further from the truth. The Law School, filled as it was with friendly colleagues, seemed cut off from the rest of the University as if by a vast moat.

For a brief moment, I thought that I had discovered a bridge to Harvard Yard when a young historian asked me to join a group of his colleagues at a weekly poker game in a smoke-filled basement of one of the undergraduate residence halls. After two disastrous sessions, however, I reluctantly concluded that I could no longer afford to communicate with the rest of the University via the gaming table. Other opportunities to widen my horizons failed to materialize, for one reason or another. And so my fondest hopes for an academic career went unfulfilled.

At that time, I had not yet discovered the philosopher's wry admonition: Take care in your youth when you choose your ambitions, for in your middle years you may achieve them. As I yearned for more contact with lively minds and intellectual activities around the University, I never imagined the scale on which my hopes would one day be realized.

Many years later, I learned that trying to keep up with everything going on at Harvard was an impossible undertaking. Modern universities are immensely complex institutions. Indeed, Clark Kerr has argued that they should be called multiversities because they are responsible for such a dizzying variety of programs and activities. Kerr undoubtedly has a point. Within the past few years, colleagues of mine at Harvard have helped to write a tax code for Indonesia, created a new program for educating medical students, conducted seminars for recently elected members of Congress, won a Nobel prize for research conducted in Geneva, taught physics to high school students in the surrounding community, briefed several heads of state on domestic and international issues, designed major construction projects in Jerusalem, written hundreds of books, given thousands of lectures, and taught tens of thousands of students.

It is the last of these activities, the teaching of students, that is the subject of this book.[1] How well do our universities edu-

1. Some readers may wonder why anyone would write about universities without discussing research. Since scholarship and scientific discovery are the most distinctive contributions of our major universities, writing a book without mentioning what goes on in the library or the laboratory may seem odd, to say the least. Yet the fact is that almost no one can write comprehensively about research. The issues that really matter are intellectual questions concerning the shifting interests, problems, and methods that mark the process of scholarly investigation. Such issues differ profoundly from one field to another and are best understood by active scientists and scholars. That is why authors who write in general terms on the state of university research so often discuss problems of secondary importance,

cate their students, and how could they do better? The importance of the subject seems obvious. Research universities enroll a disproportionate share of the most intellectually gifted high school graduates. They attract virtually all of the most talented students entering professional schools. These young people are a vital national resource, and what they learn in universities is important to us all.

Or is it? College presidents are forever making claims about the importance of education, and they are rarely contradicted in public. Yet the agreement may not be as strong as one might think. Disputing the importance of education may seem comparable to criticizing motherhood and family. But many people believe that native talent is more important than what a student learns in class; that things not learned as a student can be learned later on at one's job or on one's own; that beyond giving an adequate level of preparation, the principal function of universities is to recruit and classify talent so that it can be identified more easily by graduate and professional schools and, ultimately, by employers. These beliefs reveal why corporate recruiters inquire very little into the quality of management programs but take care to visit the universities that attract the brightest students. They help explain why law teachers spend many hours grading exams and ranking their students yet provide them with little feedback that will help them learn to do better in the future. They may even suggest why selective colleges talk so much about the SAT scores and other intellectual accomplishments of their entering classes but say so little about how much these students actually learn after they arrive.

In fact, no one knows a great deal about how much students learn in colleges and universities, and it is very difficult to find out. Cognitive psychologists are exploring the question, and

---

such as the adequacy of government support, the obsolescence of equipment, or the need to attract abler students into graduate schools. These are significant topics, to be sure, but they hardly go to the heart of the research enterprise. To write about the deeper questions of research across a wide spectrum of fields may be a task beyond the capacities of almost any author.

some of their recent research is encouraging. For example, according to Kurt Fischer and Sheryl Kenny:

> Although environmental support is required for optimal functioning at any developmental level, it seems to be especially important at the highest levels of abstraction. One of the most important roles of educational institutions may well be to provide the support that is necessary for functioning at high levels of abstraction. Indeed, people may be almost incapable of routinely using high-level skills without supportive environments like those provided by educational institutions such as high schools and colleges.[2]

Although these findings are intriguing, much more work remains to be done, and the full effects of a university education may not be known for a very long time to come. Even so, our uncertainty on this score hardly means that we should be less committed to trying to make our educational programs better. As with many issues of policy, our views about the importance of education must be based in large part on judgments rather than proven facts, judgments that depend on a prudent assessment of the stakes involved.

There are several reasons for placing a high value on education. One of them is that the problems arising in many forms of work seem to grow steadily more difficult and to require greater amounts of knowledge for their resolution. In the professions, for example, doctors have to master increasingly sophisticated decisionmaking methods and cope with difficult problems of costs, ethics, and patient psychology that were largely ignored a generation ago. Business executives confront mounting competition from abroad, more intricate questions of science and technology in their product lines and production methods, increasing pressures from government and community to help in addressing a variety of social problems. Public officials face greater

2. Kurt W. Fischer and Sheryl L. Kenny, "Environmental Conditions for Discontinuities in the Development of Abstractions," in R. Minas and Karen Kitchner, eds., *Social-Cognitive Development in Early Adulthood* (New York: Praeger, in press).

challenges now that the agencies they administer have become so huge and the problems that government tries to solve so complex. As the work required in many walks of life grows steadily more demanding, the costs of being poorly prepared must presumably rise as well.

Another phenomenon that makes the world seem more complicated is the rapid increase in the sheer amount of information to be learned. Knowing that this growth will surely continue, we can no longer be content with teaching students to remember a fixed body of knowledge; instead, we must help them to master techniques of problem-solving and habits of continuous learning. This shift makes the quality of a university education more important, not less. By and large, it is much easier to absorb a body of knowledge on one's own than it is to learn to solve problems or to master new modes of thought. Hence, formal instruction is likely to become more important and the consequences of inadequate education more serious than they have been in the past.

Increasing competition from abroad—economic, political, and military—also raises society's stake in maintaining a high quality of education. Our labor force is highly paid and our supply of raw materials no longer exceptional. More and more, therefore, the United States will have to live by its wits, prospering or declining according to the capacity of its people to develop new ideas, to work with sophisticated technology, to create new products and imaginative new ways of solving problems. Of all our national assets, a trained intelligence and a capacity for innovation and discovery seem destined to be the most important. Since universities have the principal responsibility in our society for helping to develop people who possess these capabilities, the quality of the education they offer is likely to take on greater and greater importance.

America's stake in education is also closely linked to the nature of our political system. In a democracy like ours, the quality of government depends on an informed electorate. In an era when the issues facing the society have become so difficult and numerous and the government has assumed such unprecedented responsibilities at home and abroad, the risks arising from a poorly educated population must be greater than ever before.

Beyond these practical considerations lies another reason that is no less compelling. Universities should do their best to improve the quality of their programs not only because students and society have to cope with pressing problems but also because education is important for its own sake. Professors, deans, presidents have all chosen to devote their lives to educating others. They have made this commitment because of their respect for knowledge and their desire to learn. These very reasons should impel them to do their best for their students, whether or not the practical results can ever be proven. As professionals, they owe that effort to those who pay the salaries that enable them to enjoy a life of learning. As intellectuals, they should be the first to have faith in the importance of education—not a blind faith, to be sure, nor simply a faith based on prudent calculation, but the faith Dean Inge has described as "a choice of the nobler hypothesis." If scholars must choose whether it matters if young people learn to grasp important ideas, or to appreciate great works of literature, or to reason more precisely, it would surely be ignoble to respond with anything less than a vigorous affirmation.

This is a particularly interesting time to consider the state of education in our universities, for the past ten or fifteen years have been marked by much innovation. Faculties have launched a wide variety of imaginative ventures, including experimental curricula, novel methods of instruction, and efforts to reach new groups of students. The literature on higher education teems with discussions of self-paced learning, computer-assisted instruction, core curricula, and nontraditional programs for older students. The next decade or two will determine which of these experiments will take root and which will wither away. The choices made are bound to have an effect on the processes of teaching and learning for generations to come.

Many of the pages that follow will be devoted to exploring

how universities make these choices and how they change the methods and content of their teaching in response to new opportunities and needs in the outside world. This inquiry offers a useful perspective from which to study American universities, for it is the constant pressure to respond to society's needs that most distinguishes our system of higher education from its counterparts abroad. By examining responses to past demands, we can understand how our universities became what they are. By perceiving new demands, we can anticipate how they will develop in the future.

In describing how universities evolve, I point out that they are driven to an extent unique in the industrialized world by the stimulus of competition. At the same time, the nature and results of this rivalry are quite different in education than in other fields of human endeavor. To illuminate these differences and their consequences, I consider a range of programs, starting with the core of the university—the liberal arts college—and then shifting to the professional schools, especially schools of law, business, and medicine. Thereafter, I look at some important changes currently taking place in higher education: the increasing use of advanced technology in teaching, the effort to develop better ways of preparing students for public service, and the growing interest in midcareer education for practitioners in many different professions. At the end of the book, I draw some conclusions about the performance of our universities—and suggest how they can develop in the future to make greater contributions to students and to society as a whole.

1

The American System of Higher Education

Just after I was appointed to my present position, a Harvard alumnus asked me to spend a bit of time talking to an elderly gentleman of his acquaintance. Apparently this gentleman had acquired a reputation in business circles for being unusually wise in the ways of large organizations and how they could be governed effectively. By now, the details of our conversation have grown dim in my mind—except for one unforgettable observation. "Remember this," said my venerable adviser: "your most creative ideas about the future of Harvard will come in the next few months, before you take office and get embroiled in your official duties."

What a disturbing thought! Before our conversation, I had supposed that I could spend a happy interlude getting to know members of the faculty, poking about in Harvard's many professional schools, making a few key appointments to strengthen my staff. Suddenly, it seemed, I had to have ideas—big ideas—else I would be forced to settle for an undistinguished tenure trying to hold things together without hope of making significant improvements.

As each day came to a close, I noted with a twinge of regret that another opportunity had come and gone with nothing creative to show for it. I began to wonder what my predecessors had done to take advantage of this crucial period. Looking into the matter, I found that Charles W. Eliot had lost his wife just before being chosen president. According to his biographer, Eliot finished out the term teaching chemistry at MIT and spent the summer at his home in Chestnut Hill laboring over his inaugural address. "Work was his refuge from sorrow and he worked day and night."[1] On reflection, this example seemed a bit austere for my tastes.

Eliot's successor, A. Lawrence Lowell, had already formed most of his ideas before being offered the presidency as a result of years of opposing Mr. Eliot's policies in faculty meetings. He too continued teaching after his appointment was approved. Apparently the classroom gave him a welcome forum in which to dispel groundless rumors appearing in the local press. "I am not going to instruct the Faculty to abolish football," he declared, "or to have the students study between meals."[2] So great was Lowell's enthusiasm for his new duties that he took over on May 19 instead of waiting for the fall term to begin. Again, this was not precisely the example I was looking for.

The preparation of James Bryant Conant was a different matter altogether. For Conant did something quite unexpected. Having earlier studied for a time in Germany, he elected to return to Europe for several weeks to wander about among British universities observing, talking, looking for good ideas.

Mr. Conant's example was by far the most intriguing I had discovered. And yet, reflecting on his experience, I realized how much must have changed in the intervening forty years. Despite my affection for Europe—where I had traveled while in college, studied as a Fulbright scholar, and met and married my wife—I had no inclination at all to go there now. Certainly, the trip would have been enjoyable. I would have encountered many scholars of exceptional ability and enjoyed many stimulating conversations. I simply had no sense that such a journey would bring me the ideas I needed.

1. Henry James, *Charles W. Eliot, President of Harvard University, 1869–1909*, 2 vols. (Boston: Houghton Mifflin, 1930), vol. 1, p. 224.

2. Henry Aaron Yeomans, *Abbott Lawrence Lowell, 1856–1943* (Cambridge, Mass.: Harvard University Press, 1948), p. 102.

What accounted for my attitude? Why were Old World universities no longer a model for America? I scarcely knew at that point, apart from a general impression that few striking innovations in higher education had emerged from European universities during the postwar period. The subject soon passed from my mind, only to reappear a dozen years later at a conference of European rectors in Berlin, when I began to have glimmerings of an answer.

Distinctive Characteristics of the American System

President Conant's trip abroad was quite in keeping with tradition. As a new country conscious of its roots in the Old World, America had ample reason to look to Europe for inspiration in shaping its institutions of higher learning. And look to Europe we did. From England, as long ago as colonial times, came the notion of a broadly based education in a residential setting aimed not only at training the mind but at developing character. This was the model that inspired our concept of a liberal undergraduate education. From nineteenth-century Germany came the idea of a faculty involved in research and dedicated to the preparation of future scholars. This was our model for graduate study.

Beyond these animating visions from abroad, the American university responded to domestic stimuli as well. For the most part, these influences grew out of deep-rooted values in the native culture: a distrust of government and an abiding faith in competition. Eventually, those values helped to mold American universities in special ways and endowed them with characteristics that set them apart from the European institutions that had earlier been their models.

Autonomy

One of these distinguishing features is the remarkable freedom from government control that our institutions of higher learning have enjoyed. In the United States, any group or organization can found a private college or university. During the nineteenth century, this freedom encouraged the growth of hundreds of colleges, as every religious denomination and every locality sought to have its own. By 1910, America boasted almost one thousand colleges and universities enrolling a third of a million students; in the same year France numbered but sixteen universities and forty thousand students. The passage of time has not removed the opportunities for new initiatives. From 1960 to 1980, the number of four-year institutions in this country rose from 1,451 to 1,810.

In established colleges and universities, public as well as private, faculties can appoint new professors without government review. Private institutions are free to select their own students, and their public counterparts have similar power, at least in their graduate and professional schools. Faculties can also determine their own curricula, albeit within the broad limits set for professional schools by the licensing and accrediting organizations that establish minimum standards for their calling. Private universities distribute funds as they wish among their many programs and activities, while most public institutions also have considerable discretion to allocate the money received from their state legislatures. Finally, all universities can seek funds from a variety of sources—student tuitions, state appropriations, corporate gifts, individual donations, foundation grants, federal agency awards. In this respect, the differences between public and private universities have steadily narrowed; many private colleges now receive assistance from their state governments, while public institutions have raised tuitions and have grown increasingly aggressive in seeking private gifts.

These characteristics depart radically from the pattern set in most of Europe. Consider West Germany, for example. Virtually all West German universities are established as state institutions by government charter. Almost all their funds come from public sources. The state guarantees admission to everyone who passes the *Abitur* examination on leaving high school (although in certain fields, such as medicine, the government sets limits on the number of places). If too many students apply to any single institution, public agencies decide who can attend and direct the overflow to other universities. Academic bodies can recommend faculty appointments, but the state has the right of final approval and can reject the university's choice. Indeed, civil authorities sometimes acknowledge denying appointments on political grounds, a predictable response to the highly partisan appointments process in the more politicized German universities. Government officials also decide, after discussions with university representatives, how much money should be appropriated to the university and how to allocate the funds. Even faculty salaries are fixed through direct negotiations between individual professors and state officials. Only in matters of curriculum and course content do universities and their professors have the autonomy taken for granted in America—and even then government officials can exert an influence through their power to set curricular guidelines and their control over the examinations that students have to pass in order to graduate and qualify for preferred jobs.

In exercising this authority, German officials do give great leeway to the individual professor. Faculty members in Germany have traditionally been free to teach what they want. The right is even included in the national constitution, and the state would have no practical way of controlling what goes on in the classroom even if it wished to do so. Nevertheless, public officials have responsibility for many administrative matters that universities in the United States would routinely handle themselves. Whereas American professors speak with deans and university presidents to shape their working conditions and to determine academic policy, German universities have traditionally lacked a strong campus administration, and professors negotiate directly with the government on many matters.

This state of affairs is not unique to Germany. Although practices and procedures vary from one European country to another, the government exercises broad control over basic academic functions in virtually every nation on the continent. In France, for example, "the controlling influence of State authority is still to be felt in the smallest administrative details, involving budgetary resources, facilities, premises, teaching staff and recognition of diplomas."[3] Only British universities have traditionally enjoyed an autonomy similar to ours and have developed an administration of some influence at the campus level.

Even in England, now that the national government has become the dominant source of funds for all higher education, public officials have come to exert more power than they do in this country over the growth and priorities of universities. There are recent signs of mounting government pressure in the University Grants Committee, the principal agency for distributing funds to the universities. In earlier times, the committee was a model of independence and simply allocated lump-sum grants to each institution. In the mid-1960s, however, the government moved the committee from the Treasury to the Department of Education and Science, making it possible for the department to coordinate academic programs and to fix priorities for universities. By 1985, officials were openly exerting financial leverage to further national goals by influencing the nature of funded research, the fields in which new positions for scientists would be authorized, and the relative emphasis given to different subjects in the curriculum.

Government influence has undoubtedly been growing in the United States as well. Statewide systems and coordinating bodies exercise greater power than before over the growth of public institutions. The federal government has imposed regulations on all universities forbidding discrimination based on sex, race, age, religion, or national origin in selecting students and hiring faculty and staff. Washington has also achieved such dominance in funding scientific research that federal officials could exert great control over the pursuit of science on our campuses if they chose to do so. Even so, the existence of strong

3. Louis Lévy-Garboua and François Orivel, "Inefficiency in the French System of Higher Education," *European Journal of Education* 17 (1982): 159.

independent colleges and universities, the multiplicity of funding sources for most activities apart from scientific research, and the constitutional safeguards of free speech and due process combine to give American universities greater freedom from government supervision than higher education enjoys in any other major country of the world.

Competition

The second distinguishing feature of American higher education is the extent to which our colleges and universities compete with one another—for faculty members, for students, for funds, and even for successful athletic teams.[4] There is no single goal toward which this rivalry is addressed. For struggling colleges at the margin, the aim may be to offer a reasonable education while avoiding having to close down. For a church-affiliated institution like Holy Cross or an innovative college such as Hampshire, the objective is to offer a distinctive experience to a special type of student. For major research universities, the end is greater prestige. This goal does not necessarily call for increased size or even added facilities except as these are means for attracting more eminent professors and a more academically talented student body. It is the quality of students and, above all, the reputation of the faculty that determine a university's prestige.

In pursuing their several objectives, different segments of higher education do not vie with one another in any meaningful sense. Hamilton College does not challenge Stanford, and neither of these competes with Visalia Junior College. But in the United States there are enough institutions in each category, and more than enough research universities, to permit a vigorous rivalry. The resulting competition is recorded periodically in widely publicized rankings of graduate faculties, professional schools, colleges, and even libraries. Such ratings, regularly crit-

4. I do not mean to speak of competition *among students*. On this score, several countries, such as France and Japan, have produced an intensity of competition in approaching state-administered entrance examinations that may surpass anything seen in this country.

icized but never suppressed, have hardly been known in other countries, at least until recently.

The process of academic competition is a curious one. Athletics aside, the rankings of universities, and even of professional schools, change surprisingly little over time. Virtually all of the "top twenty" institutions in 1980 were also in the top twenty in 1970, 1960, and 1950—although there have been some changes in relative standing within the group. Apparently, success attracts the abler students, better faculty, and greater funding that lead to continued success. Deterioration, of course, can occur. But in a large university, power is so dispersed among many quasi-independent units—departments, centers, schools, institutes—that it would be unusual for the relative position of an entire institution to improve or decline dramatically.

Although competition seldom brings immediate rewards, the rivalry continues to be keen. Every year, the campaign to recruit students begins again, the search for able junior faculty members starts afresh, other institutions renew their attempts to lure away one's finest professors. While these efforts seem most intense among the best-known universities, all institutions must compete, if not to better their position, at least to avoid losing ground. In times like the 1980s, when the population of 18- to 24-year-olds is declining, less selective institutions must struggle especially hard to avoid ebbing enrollments that will force financial cutbacks or even bankruptcy.

Such competition could not occur without the freedom of action that American universities have traditionally enjoyed. Conversely, competition works in subtle ways to preserve and strengthen the autonomy of the public institutions. Unlike the situation in Japan, where private universities are numerous but weak, or in Europe, where such institutions hardly exist, in the United States many private universities are highly regarded and help to establish prevailing standards of excellence. The resulting competition can often force state legislators to allow their universities to match the patterns established in the private sector in order to keep them from falling behind.

In contrast to the situation in the United States, the forces of competition in higher education are slight in most other industrialized nations. West Germany, for example, offers few incentives to compete even if universities were so inclined. There is not much sense in working to recruit the ablest students in a system where universities do not control admissions and the government awards all financial aid in a uniform manner. It is hard to compete for faculty when state officials fix all academic salaries and allow only a slight premium for professors recruited from another German university. Even the effort to innovate, to be distinctive, to build something of special quality is inhibited when educators must obtain almost all of their funding from the state with little recourse to corporations, wealthy donors, or other private sources of support.

The product of the German system is an array of universities marked by much smaller differences in quality than those commonly found in the United States. Much the same is true of Sweden and Italy. In other countries, a greater degree of hierarchy exists. In France, the *grandes écoles*, such as Normale and Polytechnique, attract the brightest students and prepare them for the most influential posts in government and business. But this is hierarchy by decree rather than a result of competition among rival institutions. Public officials have typically been reluctant to pass laws that might damage the preferred position of the *grandes écoles* and have worked to maintain their preeminence by helping their alumni get better jobs. To be sure, universities do compete to some extent, especially in recent years. Nevertheless, there are too few institutions at the top to allow real competition to occur, and the less prestigious universities have little chance of moving into the select group. The University of Aix-en-Provence, for example, has scant hope of becoming the leading center of business training even if it should aspire to that position; nor could the University of Lyon expect to build a school for public service that would rival the Ecole Nationale d'Administration.

British higher education gives the appearance of operating in a manner more akin to that of the United States. Not only do British universities have considerable autonomy; there are also wide differences in quality and prestige between Oxford and Cambridge on the one hand and most of the red brick universities on the other, not to mention the polytechnical institutions created by the government after World War II. Even so, the sense of institutional rivalry in Great Britain is attenuated, to say the least. Universities receive most of their funding from the government, and allocations are made, not by competition, but through discussions within the University Grants Committee. Individual universities are reluctant to vie with one another in recruiting the ablest students or to spend large sums to attract one another's professors. Indeed, to British eyes, the very idea of relying openly on competition to motivate and shape institutions of higher learning would seem in distinctly bad taste. As one British writer observed, in a country that lives by established traditions and privileges, an institution like Oxford "is not obliged to compete. There are no challengers perpetually ready to depose Oxford from its pre-eminent position . . . Oxford, then, unlike its American counterparts, is not out to prove itself. As an establishment institution, Oxford is an unalterable fixture in the life of the nation. This lends self-composure and dignity."[5]

In Japan, the situation is somewhat different. The vast array of public and private institutions fall into a readily distinguishable hierarchy, with the universities of Tokyo and Kyoto firmly at the top. Although this pattern seems to resemble the American one, the true nature and extent of competition in Japan are somewhat different. Competition does exist, primarily to attract better students. But private universities have been greatly underfunded, and in 1970 reached an agreement to receive up to half of their operating budget from the national government in return for giving the Ministry of Education greater control to ensure minimum standards. A handful of these institutions have managed to achieve high standards and attract

5. Christopher Rathbone, "The Problems of Reaching the Top of the Ivy League . . . and Staying There," *Times Higher Education Supplement* (London), February 8, 1980, p. 10.

good students. The majority of private universities, however, carry out little research, suffer from excessive enrollments, and have never effectively competed with the preeminent national universities, especially Tokyo and Kyoto, which enjoy the highest prestige and traditionally receive extra resources and the advantage of having their best students placed in the preferred government jobs.

Responsiveness

The independence and competition that characterize American universities cause them to pay close attention to a number of important constituencies—students, faculty, alumni, foundations, corporations, government agencies, even local community groups that can aid or impede a campus administration in its efforts to build and to acquire more land. It is especially important for private universities to be responsive, since they cannot look to the state government for much support but must continuously win the favor of students and donors or risk decline and even dissolution.

In the public sector, competition drives universities to be attentive to the same constituencies. Many state institutions are turning to alumni, foundations, and corporations with fund drives of one hundred million dollars or more; increasingly, they see such campaigns as the way to ensure continued distinction. Faculties and administrators in public institutions must compete with their counterparts in the private sector to win the grants that finance their research and provide overhead payments to defray their fixed expenses. Competition for the ablest professors likewise respects no boundaries between private and public institutions. Indeed, the latter increasingly prowl after private donors to fund "star salaries" with which to attract luminaries from other institutions. In recruiting students, coaches wage an intense competition for athletes, and several well-known state universities offer generous awards in an effort to attract a larger number of National Merit Scholars.

Universities must appeal to their constituents not only through salaries and scholarships but in other ways as well. Deans and presidents feel compelled to respond to faculty needs for housing, library facilities, reasonable teaching loads, attractive faculty clubs, even jobs for their spouses. Alumni are interested in championship football teams, opportunities for continuing education, and preferential admission for their children. Prospective students shop around among colleges, comparing their curricula, sports programs, housing arrangements, and cultural opportunities. Foundations are waited upon by campus emissaries attempting to match the interests and talents of the faculty with the priorities of professional philanthropists.

Universities abroad are not insulated from the concerns of students, employers, and other relevant constituencies. In contrast to the situation in the United States, however, the process of effecting change in Europe bears the imprint of greater government control. When constituent groups have important grievances, they frequently ignore the university administration and take their case directly to politicians and bureaucrats. These officials weigh the needs and discontents and eventually decide whether to respond, often through laws and regulations applicable to all universities within their jurisdiction. Since 1970, in an effort to decentralize, governments in Italy, France, and Sweden, among others, have created boards for individual universities that include representatives from business, labor, and other community groups. Tripartite councils of students, faculty, and staff have also been established by many European governments to share some of the power previously held by senior professors. In the end, however, these boards and councils simply represent new ways for interested constituencies to press their concerns by political means rather than by exerting market pressure.

Advantages of the American System

What can one make of our distinctive reliance on the marketplace? To many observers, there is something disquieting about the emphasis on competition and the influence of groups of constituents. The very terms seem to clash with cherished notions of learning and discovery. Whatever the language used, however, the characteristics themselves have much to recommend them as sources of motivation for those who staff educational institutions. Scientists, scholars, and university presidents are all undoubtedly animated by a desire to help their students and to contribute to learning. Still, competition provides a powerful supplement that pushes professors and administrators to perform better in the eyes of those whose opinions matter, be they students, faculty, alumni, scientific review panels, or other peer groups that evaluate scholarly quality. At the very least, these influences make a university administration continuously responsive to the needs of the groups it serves. To the extent that professors, students, and other important constituencies press for worthy ends, the competition for their favor acts as a constant spur to improvement.

Another advantage of a system responsive to many constituencies is its built-in protection against the danger of falling under the control of a single group. In many European countries, senior professors long ago came to dominate the programs, personnel, and internal organization of the university. Occasionally, as in Italy, the faculty even extended its influence into the important legislative and advisory committees that regulate higher education at the national level. Throughout the United States as well, tenured professors have become a more powerful force in enhancing the prestige of their universities and attracting funds from government agencies and private foundations. But there is a crucial difference. In Europe the senior professors have often acted to protect their own interests and to resist changes that would benefit junior faculty and students. In the United States the faculty has not used its power so conservatively, and is unlikely to do so in the future, because of the influence exerted by other audiences. An American university that went too far in catering to the self-interest of its tenured professors would soon have difficulty in recruiting junior faculty, attracting good students, and even retaining the allegiance of alumni and other donors.

As previously mentioned, many European governments have

sought to encourage greater responsiveness in higher education by creating councils composed of representatives from various interest groups. These bodies can have real influence; they participate in decisions on matters as important as appointments or curricula. Still, such political solutions have various disadvantages in comparison with the market pressures that compel responsiveness in the United States. In a market system, universities must react to outside pressures if they are to compete successfully for faculty, students, and funding. Nevertheless, professors are free to determine *how* they can best respond, so academic decisions remain in the hands of those most qualified to make them. In contrast, the representatives of different groups who serve on decisionmaking bodies often have a more questionable impact. They may be co-opted by the institution, and hence ineffective; inexperienced in academic affairs, and therefore erratic; or spokesmen for a hostile political minority, and thus destructive. Examples of all three problems have occurred in Continental universities.

Other benefits accrue from dispersing power and initiative among a large number of relatively autonomous colleges and universities. A decentralized system encourages innovation, since there are many centers of initiative and strong incentives to achieve something better. Although we have no measure to test the point, it is widely believed that American higher education produces more experimentation in teaching methods and curriculum and a greater variety of services for students than any of its counterparts abroad. Comparable benefits have come to other societies when similar conditions have prevailed. For example, Joseph Ben-David and Awraham Zloczower have observed that the period of greatest institutional development and innovation for German universities came in the first two-thirds of the nineteenth century, when higher education in Germany reached its height of decentralization and competition.[6]

A system like the American model also promotes diversity

6. Joseph Ben-David and Awraham Zloczower, "Universities and Academic Systems in Modern Societies," *Archives Européennes de Sociologie* 3 (1962): 45–62.

because it pushes institutions to carve out secure niches by serving the special needs of particular communities and groups of students. Of course, the process of differentiation does not work perfectly. The opportunity to experiment, to play a special role, exists in tension with the desire to achieve a higher status and to succeed according to the prevailing standards in the disciplines and professions. The latter pressures strongly encourage conformity. Indeed, if the criteria of success are defined too rigidly, competition may actually stifle innovation and prevent universities from adapting to meet new challenges. But success is seldom so tightly defined in this country. In such a diverse society, our colleges and universities can succeed in many different ways to satisfy many different tastes. As a result, the United States far exceeds other countries in institutional variety, with its small colleges and big universities, its religious and secular institutions, its single-sex and coeducational colleges, its public and private sectors, its vocational schools and schools of liberal arts, and other differences too numerous to mention.

A decentralized system also has a built-in protection against serious errors of judgment. All universities make mistakes, and a system given to innovation may make more than the usual number. However, when policy decisions are made at the campus level, their effects are local in scope and hence less costly. In contrast, when a single government agency decides how many professorships will be authorized, or how many doctors will be trained, or how all universities will be governed, the consequences of error are much more serious, reverberating throughout the state or even the entire country.

The advantages of a competitive, decentralized system are never so evident as in periods when large social changes sweep over universities. Consider how higher education in America adjusted to the vast increase in the student population during the 1960s. With encouragement from the federal government, existing institutions expanded and states began building new colleges and junior colleges. Eventually, almost half of America's youth were receiving some form of postsecondary education without serious or widespread overcrowding. Since thousands of separate institutions were free to respond in their own ways, the system also encountered little difficulty in taking account of the differences within a growing, increasingly diverse student population. Students could choose an institution suited to their own particular needs, while the system as a whole could absorb much larger numbers without seriously diluting the quality of programs offered at the most selective universities.

In Europe, the sudden growth in student enrollments produced many more problems. The governments that controlled the expansion of the system tried to cope with greater diversity by offering a few different types of institutions—universities, technical institutes, and schools to train teachers. But these efforts did not match the variations in type and quality that characterized higher education in the United States. Although few countries attracted even half the percentage of young people enrolled in the United States, most governments failed to increase the number of universities or expand their facilities sufficiently to meet the swelling demand. Established institutions were flooded with students of widely varying abilities and needs. The result, according to most observers, was a marked deterioration in quality and standards that persists to this day.

Similar contrasts were evident in the responses to the intense campus protests in the late 1960s and early 1970s. In the United States, student unrest rarely involved academic issues but stemmed from different problems, such as compulsory military service, racial frictions, and, above all, the Vietnam War. Despite the severity of the protests on many campuses, universities responded without the need of legislation. Mistakes were often made, but most of them were undone within a few years and rarely caused lasting ill-effects.

In Europe, student demonstrations were less oriented toward outside events, such as the Vietnam War, and more directed at discontents within the universities themselves. In several countries, students and younger faculty protested over the power and unresponsiveness of the tenured professors and later against the difficulty of finding the kinds of jobs to which university graduates had long felt entitled. As young people brought their complaints to the state, public officials responded with legislation aimed at restructuring the universities and altering their methods of governance. But the lawmakers were too remote to understand the institutions they sought to reform. In most instances, therefore, the new laws did not accomplish their purpose. At times they even created prolonged conflict and unrest, as in the case of the French, Dutch, and German legislation that delegated power over internal university affairs to committees composed of warring factions of senior professors, junior faculty, students, and sometimes even employees. In most of these countries, despite periodic reforms, the results of poorly conceived legislation are still evident today.

The drawbacks of government control have become even more obvious in Europe now that higher education has become much larger and its institutions more complex. But public authorities seem uncertain how to respond. Most European officials recognize the disadvantages of a centralized system. Several governments have actually taken steps to give more discretion to individual universities or regional groupings. Yet there are strong pressures that work against real decentralization. The legislation of the late 1960s introduced legal complexities that have greatly expanded the role of government bureaucrats and lawyers. Moreover, the continued political wrangling of the 1970s caused public officials in Germany and France to intervene and take back some of the delegated powers. In the future, spurred by financial stringency, governments in Europe may decide that master plans and tighter controls are required to avoid duplication and to link curricula and enrollments to the needs of the labor market. If so, the United States will continue to enjoy the comparative advantages of a more flexible, more adaptable system.

Drawbacks of a Competitive System

Every method for organizing human affairs has imperfections, and a competitive system of higher education is no exception.

At the very least, institutions that feel strong pressure to respond to their constituencies are bound to take on many of the excesses, the idiosyncrasies, and the blind spots of the publics they serve.

One need not look far to observe the imprint of the outside world on the inner life of the university. It is well known that salaries, perquisites, and facilities of every kind tend to be much more lavish in faculties of business and law than in schools of divinity, education, and social work, which serve less affluent professions. These differences do not reflect the considered judgments of the university but result from the priorities of donors, the competition for able professors, and other factors beyond the institution's control. Diehards may insist that there is a market at work which is somehow "correct" in imposing such distinctions. But the vast majority of educators would not agree that the differences in the support for these professional schools have a convincing intellectual justification. Nor would they try to justify such oddities as the vast football stadia that many universities build or the contrast between the huge sums awarded for cancer research and the pittances available for the study of behavioral factors that might help us discover how to reduce smoking.

There are many more examples of this kind. One's perception of their number and seriousness will vary depending on what one thinks of the publics to which universities seek to respond. Some people take such a jaundiced view of these audiences that they have a very poor impression of universities as well. Such critics come from both ends of the political spectrum. Many conservatives believe that only a minority of young people possess the intellect and discipline to appreciate liberal learning for its own sake. In their eyes, new waves of students funded by government largesse have caused curricula everywhere to succumb to fads, vocationalism, and a jumble of programs and offerings patched together to pander to every taste.

Radicals, at the other end of the spectrum, see higher education as the captive servant of a corrupt, unjust society and hence as corrupted itself. In such a world, universities exist primarily to reinforce the class system. They serve established institutions by recruiting young people, ranking them according to their abilities, and credentialling them for employers. They produce useful knowledge to consolidate the power of the ruling oligarchy. Through their scholarship programs, moreover, they perpetuate myths of meritocracy and social mobility that help blind the public to the realities of an exploitative economic system.[7]

Few of us share such a pessimistic view of our society and of the demands that various constituencies make upon our universities. After all, students are interested in a good education, foundations seek first-rate scholarship and strive to eradicate social evils, and peer-review panels try to support the best possible scientific work. Alumni care about the excellence of their alma mater and support its efforts to award scholarships, retain an able faculty, and build suitable facilities and library collections. If universities have to satisfy such constituencies as these, should we not expect that their efforts will succeed, on the whole, in benefiting society?

Most people would answer this question affirmatively without harboring serious reservations. Even so, in the heat of competition, institutions may resort to questionable methods to achieve even the worthiest goals. A notable example is intercollegiate athletics. Responding to strong demands, universities have produced programs that give intense satisfactions to thousands of participants and millions of spectators every year. Yet the excesses are only too obvious. Abetted by eager alumni, coaches and officials have bribed and cheated, even forged transcripts, to recruit the most talented athletes and keep them on the field. Worse yet, thousands of underqualified student-athletes

7. Bad as this picture is, things would not necessarily get better if universities were subject to greater state supervision. Presumably, radicals believe that universities could improve only if the society and its form of government were completely changed. In this sense, the radical critique is not an attack on our system of higher education as such; higher education is seen as only one manifestation of a fundamentally flawed economic and political system.

have been enrolled by special admission in well-known universities, which use them for four years to further the institution's athletic ambitions and then abandon them without a degree or adequate preparation for a worthwhile career. These shabby practices persist year after year, not simply because of the weakness of campus officials but also because of the pressure for winning teams exerted by alumni, students, and even state legislators—not to mention the lure of television revenues generated by enthusiastic audiences.

Unsavory methods of competition are by no means confined to the athletic field. They can also infect the academic enterprise, especially in difficult times when money and students are in short supply. In recent years, as the number of young people has declined, more and more schools have resorted to aggressive marketing techniques. Some colleges create attractive-sounding programs with little real substance. Others issue propaganda with misleading statements about the institution's own programs or with disparaging remarks about its competitors. In struggling to find support for research and facilities, universities increasingly turn to Washington lobbyists for help in obtaining funds, not through peer review based on scientific merit, but by persuading friendly congressmen to wangle appropriations on political grounds. Critics have also alleged that universities occasionally permit companies to exert too much influence over the conduct of research or agree to excessive delays in publishing research findings in order to reap the immediate benefits of a large corporate grant.

Competition, even if fairly waged, can also produce wasted effort and resources. Without cooperation or central planning, universities often authorize unnecessary programs to satisfy the faculty or to bid for institutional prestige. In the 1960s, for example, such motives led to many third-rate doctoral programs that produced far more Ph.D.'s than the nation needed. Even the most routine forms of rivalry can take a heavy toll on the energies of faculty and staff. In competing for federal grants, scientists frequently spend 10 or 20 percent of their time preparing grant applications, receiving site visits, or sitting on expert panels to review the proposals of other investigators. Increasingly, professors as well as presidents and deans divert their energies from education and research in order to raise money, talk to alumni, or speak with groups of prospective students. Countless hours are devoted to trying to lure professors from one university to another, only to provoke more hours of negotiation in the other institution to stop the threatened defection. These burdens may be well worth enduring, given the benefits of independence and competition, but it would be pointless not to acknowledge that the burdens do exist.

Similar problems result from the eagerness with which universities rush to serve their various publics. These constituencies are forever making demands and developing needs that universities try to satisfy. This tendency, in itself, is not a fault. Far from it. The willingness of our universities to respond to new needs and to experiment with new forms of service has helped innumerable people and resulted in all manner of useful innovations. Yet the desire to serve can be carried to extremes. The university may take on more peripheral tasks than it can manage. When this occurs, top officials will spread themselves too thin and begin to neglect their central task of improving the quality of education and research. Even faculty members can be excessively distracted by consulting or community service activities, leaving them less and less time to teach their classes, do their research, or simply indulge in sustained, uninterrupted reflection.

The last great problem of our decentralized, autonomous system—and the problem that most often draws criticism from abroad—is the willingness to tolerate institutions of low quality. Any college that can attract enough students to pay expenses can operate in this country, at least if it meets the minimum standards required for accreditation. These standards, though useful, are very modest, for the consequences of disaccreditation can be severe, and there are natural inhibitions and political constraints that deter officials from making frequent use of such a drastic remedy. In the state-controlled systems abroad, where governments control the budget and approve appointments, there are more numerous and effective levers for maintaining respectable standards. (This is presumably why the Japanese government, troubled by the poor quality of many of its private universities, agreed to assume up to half of their operating costs in return for greater powers to impose standards.) Such controls appear to accomplish their objective. In countries such as England, France, and Germany, one can find undistinguished universities but few of genuinely poor quality. In sharp contrast, among our three thousand colleges and universities, there must be hundreds that would not qualify in Europe as serious institutions of higher learning.

The various drawbacks of competition may seem daunting at first glance. But the situation is not exactly as it appears. Granted, the hucksterism in student recruitment, the abuses of intercollegiate athletics, and similar competitive excesses do represent costs attributable to the special features of the American system. But this is not true of the other apparent disadvantages.

Consider the charge that decentralized systems lead to oversized or overlapping programs and thereby waste resources. It is undoubtedly true that, without central direction, universities sometimes create unnecessary programs or enroll more students than the economy can absorb. What is much less clear is that central planning would improve matters. Government decisions on future manpower needs are notoriously erratic and vulnerable to political pressures from groups seeking to expand opportunities and enrollments. For example, planners in many European countries vastly underestimated the growth of student numbers in the 1960s, and public officials in Italy, France, and Germany have been unable to control enrollments to avoid heavy unemployment among several categories of university graduates. Even in the United States, the most recent and most serious gluts in trained manpower—the oversupply of Ph.D.'s in the 1970s and the growing surplus of physicians in the 1980s—were not merely products of the free market but were consequences of policy decisions in Washington to subsidize these categories of students. Problems can also result from the efforts of central planners to eliminate duplication of programs. In the short run, such efforts may appear to carve away waste. Over time, they can be harmful because it is so difficult to predict which programs will be most successful and so easy to make such decisions on political or expedient grounds. In all likelihood, therefore, considerable duplication is not only tolerable but necessary to produce the greatest intellectual progress.

The time and effort expended in vying for students and faculty can likewise appear to be a substantial cost of competition. But systems controlled by the state have heavy burdens of their own. Government regulation quickly leads to red tape and mushrooming bureaucracy. Tripartite governing councils force faculty members into endless meetings and acrimonious disputes. It would be difficult to persuade a German rector negotiating with the state bureaucracy or a French professor quarreling with students over a faculty appointment that the scholarly life is more placid under central planning.

It is also unclear whether competition drives our universities to take on more community programs than they would accept under a more centralized system. In the United States, it is not pressure from private educational institutions that has driven their public counterparts to deliver such an array of services to the community. On the contrary, the state universities, which are most subject to government control, have always led the way in finding new ways to help the public outside the normal programs of teaching and research. Probably, the willingness to perform more and more community services reflects the peculiar traditions of this country and the desire to earn the goodwill of legislative appropriations committees. The same tendencies might well exist if there were no competition.

Even the existence of substandard colleges and universities may not be as serious a drawback as many foreign critics suppose. The students educated at marginal institutions in America would not go to college at all in most other nations. It is far from obvious that depriving them of this opportunity would be preferable. A number of the colleges that would earn the scorn of European intellectuals do at least an adequate job of making up for the failings of our public schools and preparing students for occupations of their choice. This task may not seem intellectually elevated, but it is valuable just the same. Other countries might not do any better than we in maintaining high standards of quality if they undertook to educate such a large proportion of their young people. Their chances of doing so would be especially slim if their students came to them from American high schools rather than their own more rigorous lycées and gymnasiums.

All in all, the costs that are truly peculiar to the American system seem small in comparison to its benefits. A decentralized, competitive process makes universities more venturesome, more variegated, and more adaptable to changing needs. Over the years these virtues have stood us in good stead. Most experts here and abroad believe that our universities surpass those of other industrialized countries in their capacity for first-rate research, the quality of their professional education, the degree of innovation in their educational programs, and their success in opening higher education to the entire population and providing the variety to meet the differing needs and abilities of a huge student population. At a time when America is so concerned over its competitive position in the world, such achievements should be welcome news indeed. Factors other than decentralization and competition, such as the amounts of money the public has been willing to spend on universities or the influx of European scholars after the rise of Adolf Hitler, have also contributed to our success. But surely it is the peculiar nature of our system that has provided the motivation and adaptive power to stimulate constant change and improvement.[8]

8. In saying this, I do not mean to suggest that governments abroad should necessarily seek to recast their educational systems in our mold. Because American

Despite these accomplishments, our success is hardly a cause for complacency. The sad fact is that universities in most industrialized countries are in poor condition, and many of them have gotten worse in the last generation. One has the sense that higher education in Europe still has not made an adequate transition to mass education from the earlier era of training an elite for government service and the professions. Until this transition is accomplished, universities abroad will be vulnerable to such criticism that we cannot safely rely on them as a standard to judge our own performance. Instead, we will have to examine our own universities and ask how well they have adapted to our society's needs and how they might make even more valuable contributions.

In undertaking such a task, I must begin by pointing to a nagging doubt about our system. Despite the seeming advantages of competition, we cannot be entirely sure just how the competitive process works for higher education.

In many other walks of life we understand competition quite well. Professional football teams play for large stakes according to established rules, and teams of high quality develop. Auto manufacturers compete to increase their share of the market and consequently strive to produce cars that satisfy the needs and wishes of consumers. In each case, although not everyone may agree with the results, the standard of success has some claim to legitimacy.

In certain respects, the process in higher education works in much the same way. The competition for able students encourages the university administration to provide better athletic fa-

---

higher education reflects the broader culture, it is very difficult to inject our ways into different cultures and expect them to work well. For example, several governments in Europe have tried to decentralize their systems by giving more autonomy to universities, but autonomy may not work well where habits of competition, private philanthropy, and other aspects of American society are not present. Not surprisingly, such measures have often been followed by assumptions of greater central authority in an effort to save money, to link universities more effectively to the labor market, or simply to avoid destructive political squabbling among local factions.

cilities, extracurricular activities, and other services that students want and enjoy. In science, competition leads investigators to strive harder for verifiable additions to knowledge and causes universities to offer the best facilities to the most highly regarded experimenters. In both instances, competition helps to produce beneficial results: the satisfactions of the student-consumers in the first instance, and proven scientific advances in the second.

But what about scholarship in fields apart from science? Who decides whether deconstructionism is a form of literary theory with any enduring value? Or whether formal models of political theory have any promise of ever casting light on the real world? There are no reliable means of verification here, nor can we even justify the results in terms of consumer satisfaction (unless we take the rather strained approach of considering literary scholars and political theorists as consumers of their own products). It seems more accurate to regard such scholars as participants in a process where the rules are unclear and often subject to constant, sometimes acrimonious dispute. In an environment of this kind, it is much harder to evaluate the fruits of scholarship, let alone to gauge the effects of striving for reputation and prestige. To the extent that competition influences such scholars, does it merely spur them to greater efforts? Or does it make them too susceptible to intellectual fads or excessively inclined to take unorthodox positions in an effort to be "original"?

Competition may also have unexpected effects on institutions, like universities, that seek success in several different areas—scholarship, scientific research, education, student recruitment, fundraising, among others. How does the striving for prestige affect the distribution of effort and resources among these various activities? Will universities, concerned to enhance their reputations, allocate their energies and funds in a fashion that does justice to all of their activities? Can universities hope to distribute their energies optimally if some of their activities, such as research, can be evaluated much more credibly and visibly than others, such as teaching?

These musings lead to a final question especially germane to the subject of this book. How does competition affect the process of education and the development of academic programs? Clearly, it does not work in the same way here as in other fields of endeavor. Violin competitions have experienced judges whom entrants and audiences trust. Commercial products have consumers to evaluate their worth. In the world of universities, who are the arbiters who determine the standards of a good education? Students? Parents? Employers? Can any of these groups give a convincing definition of a "good" education? Do they really know how well various universities are doing in achieving the educational results they consider most important? If not, what assurance do we have that competition by universities for the favor of these groups will improve the quality of education? The more one ponders these questions, the more troublesome they seem. In the chapters that follow, they will recur again and again as we examine how educational programs evolve at college, professional, and postgraduate levels.

2

Undergraduate Education

During the months spent waiting to begin my official duties, I happened to run into an old acquaintance, an older man of wide experience who had held high posts in Washington, had served on boards of trustees, and now headed an academic institution of considerable reputation. "Could I talk with you for a few minutes in private?" he asked. "I have an idea you might want to consider, a bold step that you could take very early in your administration." "What is it?" I asked, hoping to have stumbled at last upon one of those big ideas that could apparently come to me only in these early months. My acquaintance came quickly to the point: "While you are still in your honeymoon period and people are reluctant to be critical, why not announce your intention to do away with Harvard College?"

Some cautionary instinct warned me that this proposal, though undoubtedly bold, might not be precisely the sort of creative idea I needed. I decided to play for time. "That's an unusual thought," I responded brightly. "Why do you suggest it?"

"By getting rid of the College," my companion replied, "you will clearly acknowledge that teaching undergraduates has become an anachronism in the modern university. Professors are equipped to do research and to train their graduate students to do research. Teaching introductory economics to freshmen or European history to sophomores is a waste of talented scholars who should have no responsibilities that divert them from what they do uniquely well."

Even as we spoke, I began to conjure up all manner of practical problems. Who would occupy the classrooms, live in the huge undergraduate Houses, make up the lost tuitions? What on earth would we do with the football stadium? But this was hardly the time to bring up such trifling details. I thanked my old acquaintance, and our conversation ended.

In the intervening years, I have occasionally thought again about this proposal. Apart from the empty dorms and classrooms, why did I instinctively resist its surface logic? Perhaps it was because a university without undergraduates would be such a drab institution. After all, it is the undergraduates who provide most of the energy, excitement, and exuberance responsible for the plays, the football games, the student newspapers, the musical events, and all the other activities that give so much texture and vitality to campus life.

Perhaps I also sensed then something I later learned from direct observation: how valuable it is for certain kinds of undergraduates to experience the wealth of intellectual opportunities that only a university can offer and to learn from professors who are not merely conveying the ideas of others but are themselves engaging in the search for new knowledge. For such students, active scholars and scientists, even if they are not gifted teachers, offer an authenticity, a depth of understanding, a subtlety of perception that come from constantly trying to create new hypotheses and interpretations that must sustain the weight of informed criticism.

Finally, I may have resisted out of a conviction that one of the chief virtues of a college within a university is the obligation it places on a faculty of specialists to explain their subject to talented students who are *not* specializing in the field. The necessity of making one's knowledge intelligible to an audience that is interested but unprotected by the heavy armor of disciplinary technique may be just what scholars need to connect their learning to a broader range of interests and concerns. Perhaps this is why, according to a survey taken in the early 1970s, Harvard professors regard undergraduates as the most stimulating students with whom they come in contact.

Whatever the faculty might have thought about doing away with the College, the alumni sentiment was clear. Graduates of Harvard College seemed to have no doubt where the center of the University lay. Less than twenty-four hours after my appointment was announced, an alumnus first asked me the question I was to hear over and over during the next few months: "Are you the first president who didn't go to Harvard?" "But I *did* go to Harvard," I replied, remembering my years of toil as a student at Harvard Law School and the many checks made out to Harvard University. "Of course," replied my interlocutor, smiling indulgently but conceding nothing. "What I meant was whether you were the first president not to attend Harvard *College*."

After a while, I ceased to argue the point. Instead, I took pleasure in pointing out that I was *not* the only president who had failed to go to Harvard. That distinction surely belonged to the first of my twenty-four predecessors, since he could scarcely have had a Harvard to go to. I even allowed myself to smile appreciatively when, at the following Commencement, the Governing Boards unexpectedly awarded me an honorary bachelor's degree. As several well-meaning celebrants pointed out, I had become a "true" Harvard man at last.

Why does the college count for so much in the minds of the alumni of many American universities? In Europe, after all, the undergraduate college does not even exist, and no one seems to mourn its absence. Students receive their general education in the gymnasium or lycée and enroll straightaway in some form of specialized graduate program to prepare for a career in the civil service or a profession. Even in the United States, one might have supposed that alumni would reserve their deepest gratitude for the professional schools that trained them for the vocations that shaped their lives and occupied most of their waking hours thereafter. Yet in America it is the college, far more than the graduate or professional school, that has traditionally evoked the greatest loyalties and left the most enduring memories. As Louis Auchincloss has observed: "Never again does one receive impressions with quite the same kind of emotional intensity that one does between the ages of seventeen and twenty-one. It is so brief a time, so very brief, yet one can build a lifetime on the exploitation of it."[1]

Like most institutions that arouse strong feelings, the college periodically comes under critical scrutiny from those who fear that it may be losing its way, falling from its ancient grace. Within the past two years, in the wake of a national outcry over the state of our public schools, a feeling has arisen that it is again time to examine the quality of undergraduate education. Reports have begun to appear inquiring into the value of a college education and questioning the standards that students are called upon to meet. The verdicts have hardly been encouraging. In the words of the Association of American Colleges: "Evidence of decline and devaluation is everywhere."[2] According to the Secretary of Education, in a report on the humanities: "Too many colleges and universities have no clear sense of their educational mission and no conception of what a graduate of their institution ought to know or be."[3]

There are several reasons for these harsh assessments. I have already mentioned one of them: the ability of institutions of doubtful quality to survive in our decentralized and largely unregulated system of higher education. Another contributing factor is the steady drop over the past twenty years in the academic qualifications of entering freshmen, a drop occasioned in part by the larger proportions of young people attending college in

1. Louis Auchincloss, *Yale Alumni Magazine,* June 1974, pp. 7, 9.

2. Association of American Colleges, Project on Redefining the Meaning and Purpose of Baccalaureate Degrees, *Integrity in the College Curriculum: A Report to the Academic Community* (Washington, D.C.: Association of American Colleges, February 1985), p. 1.

3. William Bennett, quoted in Malcolm G. Scully, "Endowment Chief Assails State of Humanities on College Campuses," *Chronicle of Higher Education,* November 28, 1984, pp. 1, 16.

the 1960s, and in part by the effects of television, family disintegration, and declining standards in many of our public schools. With more students arriving inadequately prepared, colleges have had to increase their remedial work at the expense of regular offerings. Changing patterns of enrollment have also had an effect on undergraduate programs. As the search for jobs grew more difficult in the stagnant economy of the 1970s, students shifted en masse from the liberal arts toward vocationally oriented studies. Faced with mounting competition for a dwindling student population, many colleges appear to have responded by relaxing academic standards, adding vocational majors, and requiring fewer liberal arts courses.

Although these cultural and demographic forces have taken their toll on the liberal arts curriculum, none of the reports criticizing undergraduate education have chosen to dwell on such causes. Rather than explain, the authors have chosen to condemn the incoherence of undergraduate programs and requirements and to discuss the kinds of courses students should take in order to become well-rounded persons fit for contemporary life. In emphasizing curriculum, the reports go beyond institutions that are struggling for survival or concentrating on vocational programs and address all colleges, including those set in research universities. The resulting criticisms raise significant questions. Are there serious defects in the quality of undergraduate education even in established universities? If so, are the problems rooted in the curriculum? Or are there other areas that need attention and promise to yield more fruitful results?

The Great Curriculum Debate

The recent preoccupation with the liberal arts curriculum is not a new phenomenon; it is this subject, above all others, that has traditionally been the focal point for educational debate both inside and outside the university. How to educate the whole person? The subject is irresistible. Students' preferences in choosing courses seem to offer important clues to shifting attitudes among our youth. In prominent universities, faculty debates over changes in undergraduate requirements are thought to give early warning of how our culture and its values are evolving.

In fact, anyone who studies the history of curricular reform since 1900 will emerge stripped of the notion that this subject holds the key to many insights about the course of American civilization. Over this period, all of the fundamental issues have remained the same. Almost every important proposal has already been tried. No permanent victories are ever won, nor are serious arguments ever conclusively defeated. Nevertheless, though new ideas are rarely advanced, the discussion *is* important. As we will discover, however, its importance does not lie in what is argued at faculty meetings or reported in the pages of newspapers and periodicals.

There are three perennial issues in discussions about the liberal arts curriculum. The first of these is how much to prescribe and how much to leave to the free choice of students. Those who argue for detailed requirements claim that college students are too young to know what subjects are truly important and too disposed toward courses of immediate or practical relevance. Those who favor more electives believe that students are much too varied in their interests to be forced into a single curricular mold. With Howard Mumford Jones, they champion "the untrammeled right of the undergraduate to make his own mistakes."[4]

While the soundest course undoubtedly lies some distance from either a wholly prescribed or a wholly elective system, it is doubtful that further debate beyond this point will ever produce a decisive outcome. Even so, like honey drawing flies, the subject continues to attract attention, especially from conservatives. In their eyes, curricular reforms that lead to fewer requirements and more student choice are seen as further victories for consumerism and fresh defeats for quality and liberal learning. Some

4. Howard Mumford Jones, "Undergraduates on Apron Strings," *Atlantic Monthly*, October 1955, p. 45.

of these critics write as if our colleges were in the midst of a long-term decline into anarchy and incoherence. This is hardly an accurate reading of our history. It is true that many institutions did relax their requirements during the late 1960s and early 1970s. But fluctuations of this kind have occurred periodically for generations. Several well-known institutions actually had fewer requirements before World War I than almost any college does today. Harvard's President Eliot, one of the greatest of university presidents, stood resolutely all his life for a completely elective curriculum. By 1900, he had pretty well carried the day. Next to his achievement, recent efforts to relax requirements seem downright puny.

The second curricular issue is how to achieve breadth in each student's education. Through decades of discussion three major camps have pressed their rival claims. One group emphasizes the transmission of a defined body of learning, often captured in a list of the great works of human thought. As Allan Bloom has put it: "Philosophy and liberal studies, in general, require the most careful attention to what are frequently called the great books. This is because [these books] are expressions of teachers such as we are not likely to encounter in person, because in them we find the arguments for what we take for granted without reflection, and because they are the sources for forgotten alternatives."[5] Another school of thought stresses an acquaintance with the principal ways by which the human mind apprehends the world—methods of understanding and inquiring about literature, art, moral philosophy, history, economy, and society, as well as physical and biological phenomena. This approach to liberal learning looks on undergraduate education as a foundation that gives students access to many fields they can pursue in later life. The third camp advocates achieving breadth by simply requiring students to take a certain number of courses in each of several diverse categories, such as social sciences, natural sciences, and humanities. This approach proceeds on

5. Allan Bloom, "The Failure of the University," *Daedalus,* Fall 1974, p. 60.

the premise that different disciplines have separate and valuable ways of apprehending the world and that requiring students to sample a wide variety will suffice to broaden their minds.

Each of these approaches has its strong, sometimes passionate, supporters. Those who believe in founding the curriculum on a central body of knowledge or a list of great books complain that students can graduate from many colleges without ever reading Shakespeare, Aristotle, or Locke. To such critics, distribution requirements are little more than "a cafeteria to cater to student tastes," while curricula emphasizing modes of thought are merely "the product of a political compromise between competing schools and departments."[6] Believers in emphasizing methods of thought agree that distribution requirements are too formless. But they protest that lists of great books are too static and arbitrary for a world in which knowledge is so vast and changes with such rapidity. Advocates of simple distribution requirements are secretly pleased by how easy they are to implement, since no one on the faculty need undergo the labor of preparing special courses. Presumably, the justification for letting undergraduates roam freely among large categories of courses is that students are mature enough to choose their own ways of achieving a broad education and will be more motivated to learn if they have the widest opportunity for choice.

If past experience is any guide, none of these points of view is likely to triumph conclusively in the foreseeable future. Instead, each will quietly incorporate some of the virtues of the others. Courses on methods of thought will take pains to include great texts on their reading lists; seminars on the great books will examine the method of inquiry employed by each author; distribution requirements will limit students to certain departmental courses that seem more important and fundamental than the others. As these adaptations occur, differences among the three approaches will blur and make a convincing resolution of the debate even less likely.

6. Bennett, quoted in Scully, "Endowment Chief Assails State of Humanities," p. 16.

The last of the curricular questions is how to achieve integration—how to teach students to synthesize what they have learned, to connect different modes of analysis and bodies of thought to illumine issues of human importance. In pursuit of this elusive goal, some colleges have relied on "Great Issues" courses in the final year. Other colleges have tried to use the senior thesis for this purpose. Some innovators have even sought to build an entire curriculum around a large integrating theme, as Alexander Meiklejohn did at Wisconsin by devoting the entire freshman year to the Golden Age of Athens and the sophomore year to American civilization.

Over the last quarter-century, all sorts of ingenious proposals for solving the problem of integration have found their way into the archives of the National Endowment for the Humanities or the files of the few foundations interested in educational innovation. Many of these ideas have attracted funds and passed into the curriculum. Increasingly, however, such experiments occur in the smaller colleges and universities rather than in the best-known institutions. In part, this trend is the result of greater specialization in scholarship. Professors dedicated to particular lines of research are reluctant to devote large amounts of time to mastering bodies of knowledge in other disciplines that bear no clear relation to their scholarly work. Only in colleges where teaching is the dominant concern of the faculty is one likely to find a large number of professors making a sustained effort to connect different fields of learning.

Many critics will deplore the incoherence of an undergraduate program taught by specialists. They will condemn the willingness of faculties to tolerate "the fatal disconnection of subjects which kills the vitality of our modern curriculum."[7] In fairness, however, we need to recognize that no one has yet progressed very far in creating a body of insights, generalizations, and concepts that will help students understand how to integrate the

7. Alfred North Whitehead, "The Aims of Education," in *Alfred North Whitehead: An Anthology,* ed. F. S. C. Northrup and Mason W. Gross (New York: Macmillan, 1953), p. 92.

learning from different disciplines and modes of inquiry. It is all very well to construct a course on energy that takes up everything from the scientific properties of coal to the policy dilemmas of saving the environment from acid rain. When the exercise is over, however, one wonders whether students will carry away any methods or insights that are useful in examining problems other than energy. What will students gain that is comparable to the capacity of an English major to understand a new literary text or the ability of an economics major to assess the consequences of future changes in the money supply or the balance of payments? If talk of achieving a synthesis has receded within the large universities, it is not because professors consider the goal unimportant but because they are not sure how to pursue it or what general concepts of integration they can offer their students.

Beneath the discussions and the rhetoric that surround the three main issues, one finds little movement toward a new vision. Still, the fact that curricular debates are inconclusive does not mean that they are unimportant. Far from it. Any college runs a serious risk if it does not undertake a full-blown review of undergraduate education every fifteen or twenty years. Properly conducted, such reviews are a way of encouraging specialist scholars to come together and consider their common aims in teaching undergraduates. The interest aroused by these deliberations will often bring more of the senior faculty into active college teaching. A revised curriculum will also entail new courses, and new courses mean that professors infuse energy and vitality into the curriculum by tearing up yellowed lecture notes and trying something fresh. Most of all, while we know that different colleges have had great success with widely varying curricula and educational philosophies, rarely has a college performed as well as it should without a faculty that believed in what it was doing. In the absence of periodic discussion and review, a curriculum loses direction and slowly grows formless. No one understands the enterprise as a whole or how one's own efforts relate to those of one's colleagues. In such circumstances, it may be wrongheaded to insist that any particular model is superior to all rival formulations. Yet a faculty that has made a considered choice of *some* common philosophy is vastly better off than one that struggles along with no philosophy at all. Whenever colleges carry on for very long without a coherent curriculum aimed at some reasonable set of common goals, undergraduate education is likely to be the poorer.

These remarks are aptly illustrated by the discussions provoked by Harvard's recent adoption of a Core curriculum. This creation was the result of much work by many members of the faculty. The final product emphasized certain basic skills and a familiarity with the principal methods of thought and inquiry. When it appeared, journalists began to publicize the new curriculum. To dramatize the story, they termed the proposal an important event for all of higher education, signaling a return to fundamentals and a redefinition of what was essential to undergraduate education. In a rivalrous academy, such approving words had the calming effect of a scarlet cape waved before a herd of pawing bulls. Piqued by what appeared to be an arrogant bid for leadership by Harvard, several critics retorted that their own colleges had long had core curricula. Others insisted that the Harvard proposal was merely a smorgasbord of warmed-over department offerings.

In the end, the controversy did little but revive old jealousies and rekindle familiar arguments. Missing from the discussion was a point that was more important, especially to Harvard. Whether or not the curriculum was genuinely novel or palatable to every taste, the debates leading to its passage did produce a common conception of a liberal education that everyone could work toward. The results were quickly apparent. After twenty years of concentrating on research, graduate training, and growth, the Harvard faculty produced more than one hundred courses for the new curriculum that were wholly original or heavily adapted from prior offerings. Students chose to enroll in these classes at a rate more than 60 percent above the levels needed to meet the requirements for graduation. More than four of every five Core courses were taught by tenured professors. Suddenly, the problem was not to cajole faculty members into teaching general education courses, but to explain to offended colleagues why their offerings did not merit a place in the Core. All of these results were of genuine value to students.

More Substantial Changes in Liberal Education

Although curricula may not have moved in any clear direction in the twentieth century, liberal arts education has changed in other significant ways. Many of these changes have come about because our store of knowledge has grown and become more specialized. New departments, such as biochemistry, have come into being, and some subjects in science that were once considered advanced are now treated as elementary. Other shifts have occurred in response to developments in the society. Courses on foreign countries and regions appear more frequently in college catalogs now that America's role in the world has expanded; offerings in women's studies, Afro-American studies, and environmental studies have emerged in the wake of corresponding social movements.

Beyond these gradual accretions to the college catalog are further developments that have altered the undergraduate experience. Most of these changes are never the subject of a committee report or a faculty discussion; they creep in almost unnoticed. Over time, however, their cumulative weight can bring about a transformation in the nature of college life. Three developments, in particular, represent important shifts in the evolution of liberal education over the past seventy-five years.

Greater Complexity

The steady increase in the amount and complexity of knowledge, along with the pervasive uncertainty over what is permanent, what is worthy of belief, what is truly important, has affected the way in which faculties describe the aims of education and the intellectual qualities they hope to foster in their students. At the turn of the century, one could find educators who proclaimed the virtues of mental discipline, others who emphasized practical skills, still others who spoke of transmitting knowledge acquired through scholarship and scientific investigation. Under each of these alternatives, however, the emphasis was clearly on conveying a large body of factual information together with a stock of accepted ideas and principles. Students could rely primarily on their powers of memory to succeed in college, and they were seldom challenged by the clash of conflicting values or confronted with problems for which there was admittedly no convincing solution.

Contrast this vision with the following passage, written in the 1970s:

> The *critical component* of education . . . attempts to expose students to multiple and conflicting perspectives on themselves and their society in order to test and challenge their previously unexamined assumptions. It strives to create conditions which stimulate students' intellectual, moral, and emotional growth, so that they may ground their skills in a more mature, humane framework of values. Critical education deliberately tries to stimulate the student to reformulate his goals, his cognitive map of the world, the *way* he thinks, and his view of his role in society.[8]

Earlier educators put great stock in what a student could gain by acquiring a sufficient body of information and by observing and emulating superior minds in action. Faculties today are likely to perceive a more difficult, changeful, complicated world in which there are many conflicting points of view and many questions without prospect of answers. In such an environment, knowledge alone is not enough; the ability to think clearly about complex problems becomes more and more important. A critical mind, free of dogma but nourished by humane values, may be the most important product of education in a changing, fragmented society.

8. Kenneth Keniston and Mark Gerzon, "Human and Social Benefits," in *Universal Higher Education,* ed. Logan Wilson and Olive Mills (Washington, D.C.: American Council on Education, 1972), p. 53.

A similar shift reveals itself in the history of efforts to teach ethics to undergraduates. Before the Civil War, the culminating experience for most college seniors was a course in which the instructor, often the president of the institution, lectured on the prevailing values of the day and applied them to important social problems and personal dilemmas. The powerful men who delivered these lectures had confidence in the values they expounded; they harbored little doubt that students could live proper, principled lives if they worked hard to apply these teachings. Toward the end of the nineteenth century, however, the study of society and human behavior began to split into many separate disciplines, and the earlier consensus on values began to break down before a complex, industrializing society. Courses on practical ethics disappeared, leaving classes in theory or metaethics that were consistent with the new belief that learning should be wholly scientific and value-free. When courses in applied ethics reappeared in the 1970s, students again had the opportunity to apply moral principles to the problems of real life. But instructors no longer expounded an accepted set of ethical norms or offered answers to important moral dilemmas of the day; such efforts would have amounted to rank indoctrination. Instead, they concentrated on teaching students to perceive moral issues and to reason about them carefully in the light of diverse ethical theories, leaving the students to arrive at answers by themselves.

Yet another illustration of the same trend appears when one looks at examinations in various subjects given at Harvard from 1900 onward. The changes over the years are particularly revealing, since examinations offer the best available evidence of what professors have wanted their students to learn. In the early part of the century, more than 90 percent of the questions merely sought to have students repeat particular facts, describe the opinions of others, or relate fixed sequences of events. "Mark on the map the routes of the French kings who went on the Crusades" (History, 1906). "Sketch and explain the action of a steam turbine of any type" (Engineering, 1905). The emphasis was chiefly on memory, and students were generally spared the task of unraveling complex problems, let alone exploring questions that had no determinate answers.

As the century wore on, the character of examinations changed. More and more questions emphasized analysis rather than memory or description: "In what respects is economics more important than politics in understanding the widespread tendency toward centralization during the fifteenth century in England, France, Germany, and Italy?" (History, 1971). By 1960, fully half of the questions in the humanities and social sciences called upon students to discuss complex problems from more than one perspective. In contrast with earlier exams, moreover, far fewer questions presupposed a single set of correct answers.

These changing objectives have been buttressed by the advent of the Xerox machine and the paperback text, advances that have transformed the kinds of material that instructors can put before their students. A generation ago, professors could ask a class to buy only one text, while possibly assigning extra library books that often went unread. In most courses, then, students concentrated on lecture notes and a single published account of the ideas and information relevant to the subject. Today, instructors can assign much more material, presenting many different points of view. In this way, current technology encourages the effort "to expose students to multiple and conflicting perspectives on themselves and their society in order to test and challenge their previously unexamined assumptions."

Extracurricular Opportunities

The second major change in undergraduate education has taken place quite outside the formal curriculum. It manifests itself in a gradual extension of the college's influence over every aspect of students' lives. By this, I do not mean that universities are regulating their undergraduates more closely by imposing more and more rules. If anything, the opposite is true. In a world that lacks any single accepted set of values, the ancient idea of *in loco parentis* no longer serves. How can a college act as a parent when parents themselves have so many different notions of how to bring up their children? What universities have done instead is to allow more freedom but to take greater responsibility for shaping the total undergraduate environment by creating more and more opportunities from which students can pick and choose to make a life for themselves at college.

One step in this process has been the growth of institutional housing for undergraduates. Almost all private liberal arts colleges now provide some sort of lodging for the great bulk of their students, and the major public universities have moved a long way in the same direction. By 1965, more than 60 percent of all undergraduates in these two types of institutions lived in buildings owned by their college or university. Over time, efforts have also been made to bring more intellectual, cultural, and extracurricular activities into the college residences. Yale, Harvard, Rice, and now Princeton, among others, have undergraduate houses with faculty mentors and a wide range of curricular and extracurricular programs attached. Other universities have created smaller dormitories built around the study of a language or a culture. Still others have arranged for faculty members and graduate student advisers to live in undergraduate residence halls.

Universities have also played an ever greater role in organizing extracurricular activities of all kinds. While such pursuits were not unknown in the nineteenth century, they have constantly grown in number and variety. Colleges have sponsored more and more intercollegiate athletic teams, created comprehensive intramural programs, and, more recently, offered recreational instruction to teach "lifetime" sports from tennis to whitewater canoeing and Kung Fu. No self-respecting college would dream of doing without dramatic societies, orchestras, bands, singing groups, and other cultural activities to fit every taste and talent. Nor would it be fitting to ignore programs for students interested in debate, community service, international relations, politics, and a lengthening list of other pursuits.

Universities have likewise extended their influence over the lives of students by expanding their counseling services. Academic advice has always been available. Yet forty years ago, even a leading liberal arts college might employ only a part-time psychologist. Today most campuses provide an array of counselors and psychiatrists who minister to more than 10 percent of all undergraduates at least once during their four years of college. Many campuses employ chaplains to respond to students' spiritual needs. Experts are available to test student aptitudes, assess learning difficulties, and counsel students on the management of time and stress. Athletic departments even supply tutors to help student athletes with their academic needs.

Another area of students' lives that comes increasingly under the university's influence is employment, during and after college. A rising number of undergraduates find work within the institution, especially now that Congress has subsidized campus jobs through the federal work-study program. In addition, universities do more and more to help students plan their lives during the summer and after graduation. Counseling is offered on how to look for jobs or apply to professional school. Mounds of documents are available to describe educational and vocational opportunities. Employers flock to the campus to give interviews. Increasingly, universities go beyond mere advice, giving funds for summer study and postgraduate fellowships abroad, developing internships in Washington and in state capitals, or even enlisting alumni in finding work for students overseas. Alumni, too, will often look to their alma mater for employment advice (as well as for midcareer education of a vocational kind), thus extending the reach of the college far beyond the normal undergraduate years.

In part, this ambitious effort to serve reflects a simple desire to respond imaginatively to the needs of students. Over time, however, extracurricular programs have come to be seen not merely as useful services but as an integral part of the educational process itself. Educators point to the dangers of a college that stresses only learning and cognitive skills while ignoring opportunities for students to engage in cooperative activities in which each relies on the efforts of others and is relied upon by others in return. Extracurricular activities, be they athletic teams or student newspapers, drama organizations or musical groups, have emerged as important means to overcome this problem. More and more, they are regarded not only as a source of enjoyment but as ideal experiences for learning to cooperate and take responsibility for the welfare of one's peers.

Like extracurricular activities, other university services have come to be seen as important influences on students' personal growth. The placement office is not just a source of information about jobs but a center for helping students to test their strengths and weaknesses and to develop lasting interests. Psychiatric counseling is perceived not merely as treatment but as a stimulus to personal growth and maturity. In these ways, a rationale emerges to justify the provision of more and more services. The contemporary college or university does not concentrate only on formal education; it assumes the larger responsibility of promoting human development in all its forms.

The Changing Mix of Students

The third major trend in liberal arts education is a steady movement toward a more diverse student body. This shift has revealed itself in many ways. Private colleges recruit vigorously to fill each class with a wide variety of talents, including musicians, actors, student leaders, writers, and athletes. Both public and private institutions have built up their financial aid resources, with help from the federal government, so that they can attract more applicants from poor and lower-middle-class backgrounds. In a few colleges, at least, alumni help to seek out students from all areas of the country. Since the late 1960s, racial diversity has added a prominent new theme to college admissions, with the combined proportion of Hispanic, black, Asian, and Native American undergraduates now exceeding 10 and sometimes even 20 percent of the student body in most university colleges. Foreign undergraduates have also grown more numerous, totaling almost two hundred thousand throughout the United States by 1985. All in all, these shifts amount to a massive transformation in the texture of undergraduate life across the nation. Fewer colleges today have student bodies that are distinctively homogeneous; almost all seek a heterogeneous enrollment reflecting a wide variety of backgrounds, races, and talents.

In the wake of these changes, patterns of student living have also altered appreciably. Coresidency has swept the nation, bringing women and men together under the same roof in the vast majority of colleges. Attempts by militants to create separate living units for black students have met with vigorous resistance. Barriers based on sex, race, religion, or social class have steadily receded, not just in university dormitories but in student-operated clubs, fraternities, and sororities as well. In recent years, a growing number of private colleges have gone still further and closed fraternities and residential clubs, replacing them with living units that include a more representative cross-section of the student body.

In one sense, these developments are responses to the familiar social pressures that condemn all forms of discrimination and favor equal opportunity and access. Once again, however, the universities have not merely adapted; they have altered their educational philosophies to embrace these changes as important steps in fostering student development. Increasingly, educators emphasize how much undergraduates have to teach one another, a sentiment that again accords with the gradual breakdown of established values and universally accepted ways of looking at society. In a world of "multiple and conflicting perspectives," better that students come from the widest range of backgrounds and bring the greatest variety of experience with them so that they have more to share with one another. And if this sharing is a vital part of the educational process, then any barrier is suspect that diminishes variety by segregating students into homogeneous groups with narrow backgrounds and interests. Coresidency becomes a virtue; even fraternities can appear to be a suspect enclave of exclusivity.

Skeptics may dismiss such explanations as rationalizations after the fact, but that is too facile. A number of universities proclaimed the educational values of diversity before the movement toward equal opportunity became pronounced. Private colleges that risk alienating their students and alumni by moving to abolish fraternities are plainly not acting from opportunistic motives. Nor would universities have supported coresidential living, no matter how much students clamored for it, had its popularity not reflected a genuine desire among students to foster more natural and rewarding relationships between male and female undergraduates. What colleges have done is to embrace a broader educational philosophy that looks on diversity and greater student interaction as important elements in a full undergraduate experience.

The Goals of Liberal Education

This expansive view of education reflects a set of established goals that is remarkable for its variety and breadth and ambitious in its hopes for the personal and intellectual development of the students. To cite the most common aims: Undergraduates should acquire an ample store of knowledge, both in depth, by concentrating in a particular field, and in breadth, by devoting attention to several different disciplines. They should gain an ability to communicate with precision and style, a basic competence in quantitative skills, a familiarity with at least one foreign language, and a capacity to think clearly and critically. Students should also become acquainted with the important methods of inquiry and thought by which we acquire knowledge and understanding of nature, society, and ourselves. They should develop an awareness of other cultures with their differing values, traditions, and institutions. By having the chance to explore many opportunities, they should acquire lasting intellectual and cultural interests, gain in self-knowledge, and ultimately be able to make sound choices about their future lives and careers. Through working and living with a wide variety of fellow students, they should achieve greater social maturity and acquire a tolerance of human diversity. Last but not least, they should enjoy their college years or at least look back on them later as a time when their interests and enthusiasms were engaged in a particularly memorable way.

These objectives express many laudable aspirations. But stating goals is one thing and accomplishing them quite another. How much do we know about the success colleges actually have in achieving this impressive list of aims?

That is a difficult question to answer for several reasons. It is hard to devise adequate tests to measure progress toward many of the goals I have mentioned. Even the ability to write is partly a subjective matter, and qualities such as moral reasoning and skill at working with others seem to defy efforts at exact measurement. Investigators have shown little interest in trying to discover how long students retain whatever they gain in college, perhaps because it is so difficult to disentangle the effects of college from those of all the other experiences college graduates have. Finally, it is hard enough to measure the progress college students make but infinitely harder to ascertain how much more progress undergraduates make than they would have made had they gone to work or had some other kind of experience. Very few studies have tried to compare college students with matched samples of young people who did not go beyond high school. Such a task would not be easy in any event. The very fact that one group chose to attend college and the other group did not suggests differences in outlook and motivation that could serve as well as the college experience itself to account for any variations in the intellectual progress of the two samples.

Because of these problems, the evidence we have about the effects of college comes from several sources, none of which is perfect: one or two inquiries comparing students who went to college with those who did not; numerous studies using tests of varying reliability to measure progress toward a spate of goals, such as substantive knowledge, mathematical ability, or critical reasoning; and opinion surveys of alumni asking what they *think* they gained from their college experience. After a detailed review of this evidence, Howard Bowen offers the following conclusions:[9]

The largest measurable increase occurs in the acquisition of substantive knowledge. Bowen estimates that four years of college probably make a positive difference of a full standard deviation. That is, students progress to a point at which the average senior has acquired as much information as the amount possessed by students at the 16th percentile of the freshman class.

Students achieve moderate gains (of half a standard deviation or slightly more) in verbal skills, appreciation and understanding of literature and the arts, and the cultivation of lasting interests and receptiveness to ideas.

According to several tests, undergraduates gain only slightly in critical thinking, but the results achieved by different investigators have varied so widely that one wonders what to make of the results. For what it's worth, alumni opinions are more positive on this score. Large majorities ranging up to 75 percent or more of college graduates feel that their ability to think improved "very much" or "quite a bit."

Quantitative skills seem to increase substantially for students who major in mathematics or use it frequently in their courses. Other students, who merely take introductory courses in math, fall quickly back to levels of competence similar to those they possessed when they entered college.

Students seem to record significant increases (of close to a full standard deviation) in their awareness of their own interests, abilities, and limitations. They show smaller but still significant growth in the level of their personal and career aspirations.

Undergraduates also make significant gains in tolerance for other points of view and show corresponding declines in prejudice, dogmatism, authoritarianism, and ethnocentrism. At the same time, there is no indication that college has had much success in increasing kindness, sympathy, altruism, or friendliness toward others.

9. Howard R. Bowen, *Investment in Learning: The Individual and Social Value of American Higher Education* (San Francisco: Jossey-Bass, 1977), pp. 63–136.

Severe problems of measurement make it impossible to say anything reliable about changes in moral sensitivity or character. Interestingly, however, graduates looking back tend to believe that college had little effect on them in these respects.

Finally, various studies lend support to the prevailing belief that the extracurricular environment can play an important role in achieving the goals of a liberal education. Several investigators have reported that students in residential colleges gain significantly more than commuting students in self-awareness, tolerance for others, and interpersonal skills. One inquiry at Harvard explored the relationship between all extracurricular activities and the degree to which students lived up to their academic potential. According to the findings of this study, the students who fall furthest below their apparent capacity are those who do not participate at all in outside activities and a smaller number who allow themselves to become hopelessly overcommitted to extracurricular pursuits. Between these extremes, the more that students engage in outside activities, the better they perform in relation to their abilities.

The Harvard study lends support to the theory, advanced by Alexander Astin, that the more actively undergraduates are engaged in any and all aspects of the college experience, the more they develop at college.[10] According to this view, extracurricular activities rarely compete with coursework in a manner that hurts academic performance. On the contrary, within reasonable limits, involvement in such activities seems to improve the self-discipline of students and increase the intensity and quality of the effort they devote to academic pursuits.

What Is to Be Done?

The findings I have just reviewed suggest that efforts to improve our colleges have produced only modest results in helping students progress toward the academic goals of a liberal education. It is hardly a cause for celebration if the average senior knows only as much as students at the 16th percentile of the freshman

10. Alexander Astin, *Achieving Educational Excellence* (1984).

class, and disturbing to learn that studies indicate much lower rates of progress in critical thinking and expository writing. Of course, it is always possible that some or all of these studies are methodologically flawed. But the findings themselves are not terribly surprising. The fact is that colleges work hard to provide new facilities, activities, and services but devote remarkably little time to deliberate efforts aimed at improving student learning.

Many educators will hotly dispute this assertion. After all, they will retort, what are deans and faculties doing when they revise the curriculum and develop new majors if not improving the quality of education? What are individual professors doing when they create new courses and labor to make old lectures better? This reaction is understandable. But the fact remains that the time faculties and administrators spend working together on education is devoted almost entirely to considering *what* their students should study rather than *how* they can learn more effectively or *whether* they are learning as much as they should. The professors who vote for new majors or curricular reforms know very little about whether these initiatives will actually help students progress toward the educational goals of the institution. And rarely, if ever, do they make a serious effort to find out.

Within the last few years, however, interest in these topics has emerged from a new quarter. Public officials have suddenly become concerned to discover how much students are learning and what benefits result from expensive undergraduate programs. To quote Secretary of Education William Bennett: "The Department of Education has an obligation to the students it assists with financial aid, and to the taxpayers whose funds it disburses, to suggest better means by which the higher education consumer can be confident he is purchasing a sound product."[11] As costs continue to rise, more and more legislators are echoing these sentiments by calling for some form of assessment

11. William Bennett, Address before American Council on Education at Miami Beach, October 28, 1985.

of how far students have progressed and whether they are fit for graduation or for advancement to a higher level of education.

The easiest way to satisfy such concerns is to require students to take a standardized test at stipulated intervals in their undergraduate program. This is what several states, including Florida and Tennessee, have already done. But standardized tests have serious drawbacks. If they are easy to pass or if little turns on the outcome, neither students nor faculty will pay much attention and the exercise will be a waste of time. If the tests are hard and the results have significant consequences—determining whether students are allowed to graduate or how much money the university will receive from the legislature—the effects may actually be detrimental. Faculty and students will begin to direct their teaching and studying toward successful completion of the exams. While this will help to ensure that students achieve minimum competence, no standardized test yet devised can do justice to the many aims of undergraduate education or even provide a decent measure of its most important objectives. Typically, such exams emphasize the acquisition of facts and the mastery of simple skills. As currently constructed, they are not suited to measuring how clearly students think about issues of social justice, how deeply they can appreciate a painting or a literary text, how much they have gained in intellectual curiosity, how far they have come in understanding their own capacities and limitations. In the end, therefore, a heavy emphasis on uniform tests threatens to trivialize undergraduate teaching and to rob it of diversity by orienting instruction too heavily toward a single imperfect means of measurement. Such a policy will not interest the faculty, let alone the abler students, and hence will not encourage a broad-based effort to enhance the quality of education.

A successful strategy of reform must enlist professors in individual institutions to work together to improve not just the curriculum but the process of learning as well. Such efforts are distressingly rare. In one small corner of American higher education, however, faculties have made a remarkable attempt to formulate common goals and work collaboratively to achieve them. These colleges are not among the better known; together they make up less than one percent of all our institutions of higher learning. Still, their experiences offer the closest approximation we have to a determined, comprehensive effort to increase the effectiveness of undergraduate instruction.

All of the institutions in question have embraced a concept called competency-based learning. All of them have begun by formulating a clear definition of educational goals expressed as competencies. For example, Alverno College—a pioneer in the movement—has adopted the following aims for its students.

1. Develop effective communications skills.
2. Improve analytic abilities.
3. Strengthen problem-solving capacities.
4. Develop the ability to make value judgments.
5. Improve facility in social interaction.
6. Achieve understanding of the relationship between individual and environment.
7. Develop awareness and understanding of the contemporary world.
8. Develop understanding of and sensitivity toward the arts and a knowledge of the humanities.

Faculty members work together to determine the criteria by which to measure these competencies and to devise the means by which each may be assessed. These methods are often unusual, calling on students to perform demanding tasks rather than simply take written exams. The actual evaluation of students is usually performed by someone other than the professor teaching the class, and all students must pass in order to graduate. Thus, instructors do not give exams, let alone rank the students by awarding a standard distribution of grades; the professor tries to help all students to demonstrate the desired competency at the highest possible level.

A system of this kind can produce major shifts in the behavior and motivations of the faculty. Much effort goes into defining common objectives and discovering reliable methods to assess them. Instructors spend a great deal of time trying to figure out how to improve the performance of their students. Because performance is measured by outside assessors using external criteria, professors lose much of their autonomy and must adapt their teaching to satisfy goals other than their own. Their success in doing so is made visible with each new round of assessments, so that those who fall short are constantly motivated to review their efforts and to find better ways of helping their students learn.

One can predict that faculty members in a research-oriented university will strongly oppose such a system. They will shrink from the prospect of endless discussions of aims and assessments and recoil from the thought of having to adapt their courses and teaching methods to serve criteria and goals determined by others. Most professors are working hard preparing new generations of scientists and scholars and trying to make important contributions to knowledge in addition to teaching undergraduates. But competency-based learning is not designed for busy people with multiple tasks. It is—at least in the initial years—an all-consuming enterprise.

Thoughtful faculty members will also wonder whether any system aimed at a single set of goals can hope to capture all the values of a liberal education. Most professors have subtle purposes and interests of their own that will rarely be included in a list of shared objectives. These individual contributions give life and texture to education and often leave a more lasting impression than any planned, collective effort can succeed in doing. In a program of competency-based learning, however, it will be difficult to keep these personal elements from being submerged beneath the overriding preoccupation with achieving common institutional aims.

In addition, even the most familiar, basic goals often elude measurement by existing methods. How is one to trace the effects of college in developing lifelong intellectual and aesthetic interests? What group of competent philosophers would agree on methods for measuring moral development? These problems afflict every attempt to assess the value of education by a common set of objectives. Such efforts have the virtue of focusing faculty attention on the task of defining common aims and determining how much progress students are making toward these objectives. The danger is that they will concentrate faculty attention on a few measurable goals to the neglect of other purposes too intangible to assess by known methods of evaluation.

A closely related objection to competency-based learning has to do with the way in which one conceives the value of knowledge. Is the study of philosophy or cultural anthropology simply a means to some collective goal, a mere vehicle for achieving a heightened capacity for critical thinking or a greater understanding of the individual's relation to the environment? Or is there a value simply in knowing about philosophy or anthropology for its own intrinsic worth—as an end rather than a means? Most faculty members believe passionately in knowledge for its own sake. This belief may strike some people as effete. But it accounts for much of the enthusiasm professors feel toward their disciplines, for many of the books that have attracted lasting attention, and for most of the basic scientific discoveries that have eventually led to useful applications. In stressing the acquisition of basic skills, therefore, competency-based learning can easily come into conflict with the deepest feelings professors have toward their subjects.

These objections seem weighty enough to dim the prospects of competency-based education as a model for most universities. Yet the status quo is not satisfactory either. By failing to articulate the shared objectives of a liberal education or to discuss how they are related to individual courses in the curriculum, faculties can easily lose sight of their common purposes. In such an atmosphere, important aims acknowledged by all, such as the ability to communicate precisely or to reason carefully, remain the responsibility of no one. Faculty members, intent upon their private purposes, may teach in ways that do little to help their students make progress toward these basic goals.

In sum, it is inappropriate and unrealistic to expect professors to subordinate everything to helping students achieve a set of shared objectives. But it is equally wrong for faculties to pay no attention to common goals and to ignore the question of how well these aims are being realized. What we need is a middle way that avoids both of these extremes.

How might such a program look? A logical first step would be to define a set of shared objectives toward which to orient teaching and learning throughout the four undergraduate years. Fortunately, it is probably not impossible to formulate a number of goals that will command wide agreement in the faculty, so long as no one insists that they be exclusive. Most professors, for example, would accept something close to the aims I described earlier in this chapter. Certainly, few could deny that critical thinking, clarity and style in communication, and acquaintance with important fields of knowledge and modes of thought are all important aims for a liberal education.

Agreement on objectives, though indispensable, is not enough; the goals must be connected in some deliberate way to the teaching of individual courses. To achieve this, several steps seem especially important. Colleges must communicate the goals to students and explain their importance. Members of departments or instructional programs need to come together and discuss ways of adapting their teaching and assignments to make sure that the shared purposes are not forgotten amid the private aims and interests of individual professors. Faculty members should cooperate to devise ways of crafting examinations to reinforce their common aims, since exams have such a strong influence on the ways students study in their courses. Finally, faculty members should give students prompt and ample feedback on their papers and exams in order to help them understand what constitutes superior performance and where their own strengths and weaknesses lie.

Although these steps seem obvious, they are rarely achieved in research universities. One can examine the catalogs and brochures of many institutions and never find a detailed description of the common goals of undergraduate education. Professors seldom meet at any length to discuss how to adapt their teaching to achieve shared objectives. The crafting of exams is almost never a topic of serious discussion; instead, faculty members typically draft their questions almost instinctively, using as models the tests they have observed over the years. Feedback on papers and exams also leaves much to be desired. In university colleges, much of the grading is left to graduate students, and comments are often perfunctory or nonexistent.

What accounts for these practices? Perhaps the answer lies in the attitudes with which faculty members approach their work. Professors are among the most independent of all professionals and guard their autonomy closely. While they are happy to discuss what courses should be required, they are suspicious of initiatives that could limit their freedom to decide how to teach or to evaluate their students.

Such attitudes help us to understand why it would not be feasible to *prescribe* collective goals or teaching methods. They do not explain why there is so little *discussion* of ways to improve the educational process. Experience, even in the most independent research faculties, suggests that deliberations of this kind are not impossible. For example, in considering its Core curriculum, the Harvard faculty adopted rather precise goals and criteria for each category of required courses and established a standing committee to ensure that all such offerings would satisfy the agreed-on standards. Compared with these measures, voluntary discussions of common goals and methods of achieving them can hardly seem terribly threatening.

Another hypothesis is that faculty members in research universities are simply too busy and too committed to their scholarly pursuits to spare the time to come together to consider how to make their teaching more effective. This is the favorite explanation of most writers who criticize educational practices in universities. Yet the criticism is usually overdrawn. There is an implication that professors are selfish and intent only on enhancing their scholarly reputations, with little acknowledgment of the intense effort required to serve simultaneously as undergraduate teachers, mentors of graduate students, and scholars seeking to enlarge knowledge and understanding. In stressing the virtues of effective pedagogy, moreover, critics often fail to recognize the immense importance of research, not just in contributing to the general store of knowledge but in helping to sustain the vitality of professors by ensuring that they continue to have something of genuine importance to teach.

No one can deny that research and graduate training do limit the time available to improve the quality of undergraduate education. Even so, the effort required to discuss educational goals or to consider better ways of pursuing them through teaching and examining is hardly so great as to rule out the enterprise entirely. The work involved is a tiny fraction of what professors already devote to teaching. It could be accomplished several times over in the hours saved from faculty meetings on much less important topics.

The problem of feedback is more complex. Unlike the other steps just described, careful evaluation of students' work can be very time-consuming and hence could interfere significantly with research and other important tasks. Still, there are ways to reduce the time involved. Graduate students can be trained to give detailed, helpful comments on papers and exams. Professors can distribute model answers or prepare written analyses of each question discussing the ingredients of a competent answer and explaining why each element is important. Computers will vastly increase the possibilities for immediate feedback. Even these initiatives may take somewhat more time than faculty members normally give to the examining process. Nevertheless, the extra burden need not be great, and there are few efforts professors can make that are more likely to enhance the progress of their students. Unless undergraduates can learn where they have not done well and why, they are unlikely to discover how to do better.

In sum, none of the obvious explanations gives an adequate reason for failing to make a collaborative effort to improve the quality of education. At best, the prevailing theories suggest why such efforts will not occur spontaneously. They do not rule out a successful attempt by a resourceful dean or department chairman to get the necessary discussions under way. The question, then, is not why such initiatives must fail but why they have been tried so rarely.

Beyond making these efforts, it is also important to devise ways of estimating their success. At present, universities have no adequate way of measuring the effects of undergraduate education or assessing the methods of instruction they employ. This is a serious defect. No human endeavor can progress, except by chance, without some way of evaluating its performance. Only with assessment of this kind can faculties proceed by an intelligent process of trial and error to improve their educational programs.

Attempts to examine the quality of education are hardly unknown. Psychologists have already produced an extensive literature on the subject. I have mentioned the many studies that try to measure the progress students make toward familiar educational goals. Investigators have also probed such interesting topics as the impact on learning of small classes and the effects of computer-assisted instruction and other new methods of teaching. The critical point, however, is that such inquiries rarely come about at the behest of curriculum committees or academic deans. The investigators are typically psychologists or professors of education who work for their own professional purposes; they rarely have close contact with campus officials who might profit from their studies. Without a connection between investigators and decisionmakers, such research lacks prestige, and much of it has no practical value for those who actually help to shape educational policies. Again and again, surveys and tests measure attitudes and changes that are of no great interest to faculty members. Most of the studies examine public school classes, and even those which focus on colleges are often of limited usefulness because they look at institutions too different from one's own for their results to have any practical utility.

What explains the failure to carry on an effective evaluation of undergraduate education? The most likely answer is that such research can seem so threatening. It may question teaching methods that professors have used for many years and thus discredit countless classes that can never be reclaimed and done over. It may signal a need for new techniques of instruction or new types of courses that will require long hours of effort. Since faculty members do not place great faith in the reliability of such research, they fear that they may be asked to spend much time introducing reforms based on studies that later turn out to be worthless. Worst of all, investigators may simply cast doubt on the value of undergraduate teaching without finding a remedy, thus calling the entire enterprise into question.

The result is a kind of vicious circle. Apprehensive about educational research and skeptical of its validity, faculties give the work such a low priority and status that their skepticism becomes self-fulfilling. To break this cycle, someone will have to take the initiative to bring educators and investigators together in a common effort to investigate questions of genuine importance to the development of educational policy in our colleges.

The most basic need is to develop serviceable methods for measuring students' progress toward common educational goals. Granted, such methods must be used with caution to avoid any risk of pushing faculty members to concentrate on what is measurable at the expense of more intangible goals. Properly used, however, adequate measures could serve to compare the effectiveness of different methods of teaching, varying class sizes, or different undergraduate majors. Such measures could also help in identifying groups of students whose progress was especially rapid or especially slow, so that investigators could seek explanations for these differences. Eventually, nourished by more basic research in human cognition, faculties might come to understand how particular teaching methods work differently for different groups of students and why some students have more difficulty than others in developing intellectually.

If studies of this kind were encouraged, would it be realistic to expect useful findings? Not in every case. I have already mentioned the difficulty of finding serviceable methods for measuring students' progress. Even when this obstacle can be overcome, it is often harder than one might think to arrive at conclusions that will inform educational policymaking. For example, consider the attempt to decide whether small classes are more conducive to learning than large classes. One might suppose that clear differences would emerge from comparisons of the performance of students in courses of various sizes. But it turns out that class size affects different students in different ways, that much depends on the type of material being taught, and that even more turns on the methods of instruction used. Sorting out these variables to arrive at useful results is no easy matter.

These difficulties do not mean that we must abandon all hope of useful results for the indefinite future. Some issues are easier to explore than others. Moreover, it is not necessary to achieve results with the accuracy required by scientific journals. It is helpful simply to arrive at conclusions plausible enough to support academic reforms. By this test, there are certainly ways of making useful assessments, even in the short run, that will give us findings more reliable than the intuitions and impressions that sway most educational debates at faculty meetings.

An example or two may make the point more clearly. At Harvard, freshmen and seniors were asked to write a short essay, and their papers were compared. A careful reading disclosed that although seniors in general seemed to have improved the quality of their writing, many science majors had actually regressed. Further inquiry suggested a persuasive explanation for this result. In most science courses, students had good reason to consider it a waste of valuable time to write complete sentences. The important thing was to state the correct formula or phrase to solve the problem and to write it as quickly as possible. Apparently, four years in such a system undermined the quality of a student's writing. Of course, this finding was hardly airtight. The assessments of student writing were admittedly subjective, and the hypothesis may not have been proven according to strict research criteria. But the conclusion seemed plausible enough to convince faculty members to change the written assignments given to science majors.

In another study at Harvard, undergraduates who took the huge introductory economics course were tested a year later to discover what they remembered. The tests showed that students had forgotten most of the terms and nomenclature but still understood the concepts and methods of analysis. Students also reported that they spent little time applying what they had learned by reading articles about economic issues in newspapers and magazines. On the basis of these results, course materials were revised to emphasize concepts and to weed out less important items of nomenclature and terminology. At the same time, instructors converted their problems and illustrations from the traditional abstract variety to contemporary questions that might enhance the students' interest in current economic issues. Once again, findings that lacked scientific rigor were persuasive enough to produce changes in teaching methods.[12]

Having surveyed the evolution of undergraduate education and examined the problems involved in evaluating its effectiveness, what verdict can we reach concerning its quality? Clearly, our conclusions must be mixed. As I suggested earlier, America does remarkably well in providing a wide assortment of educational experiences. Colleges come in many sizes and many levels of difficulty. There are denominational institutions for students of a strong religious bent, experimental colleges for students with

12. Other methods are available to produce immediate results while the search for more sophisticated measures goes forward. For example, investigators can ask students to indicate how much they *think* they have progressed toward various goals of undergraduate education and then search for patterns of study and activity that seem to explain why different groups of undergraduates feel that they did particularly well or particularly poorly. In large courses, it is possible to assign students of similar abilities to different sections and then compare their grades to determine whether differing methods of instruction or variations in class size have an effect on levels of achievement.

special inclinations, programs of study to fit virtually any intellectual interest. One could hardly ask for more variety to satisfy a vast, heterogeneous student population.

Colleges, certainly university colleges, have also done exceptionally well in providing undergraduates with facilities, activities, and services of every kind. By responding to so many kinds of personal needs, colleges have helped their students to develop, both socially and intellectually, and have increased their ability to work with others. They have also encouraged students to enlarge their tolerance and appreciation for differing backgrounds, values, and points of view. Not least, they have made the undergraduate years a happy and a memorable experience for large majorities of their alumni.

The record of our colleges in developing their curricula is much more difficult to assess. Certainly, faculties have shown themselves capable of adapting reasonably well to the shifting interests of their students. Yet what this responsiveness has meant in the last fifteen years is a large expansion in preprofessional and vocational majors and a sharp increase in the number of electives students are allowed to take. Since these trends have occurred at the expense of the liberal arts, many educators—at least the more vocal ones—have attacked the results as shortsighted and unfortunate.

These critics make a persuasive argument. Granted, students who do not wish to pursue their studies beyond the bachelor's degree have a legitimate need to take courses that will prepare them to make a living. It is hard to fault them for preferring a vocational major instead of concentrating in literature, philosophy, or some other liberal arts discipline. At the same time, many undergraduates wrongly assume that they need to accumulate preprofessional courses in order to maximize their chances for admission to the professional school of their choice. Many colleges have allowed vocational majors to claim more than 60 or even 70 percent of the courses that undergraduates can take during their four years. In these respects, at least, recent trends seem to have pushed professionalism beyond reasonable bounds, to the detriment of other dimensions of a full life that are the special concern of the liberal arts. Some may defend these trends by arguing that they reflect the personal choices of students. But such a market test is more suitable for judging breakfast cereals and cosmetic products than for evaluating educational programs. Only a dedicated libertarian would insist that college students are experienced enough to choose all their own courses and to balance their vocational needs against the other dimensions of human existence to which the undergraduate experience can contribute. For most educators, then, the free market is hardly a guarantee of the best possible curriculum.

In evaluating the state of undergraduate education, one must be careful not to exaggerate the significance of the curriculum. It is important to conduct a review at suitable intervals in order to achieve *some* reasonable set of requirements and *some* clear set of educational goals that will unify and inspirit the faculty. But curricular debates only involve the arrangement and rearrangement of individual courses and do not touch upon the ways in which professors organize their material, teach their classes, and examine their students. Hence, the fascination with curriculum, so typical of American undergraduate education, protects traditional faculty prerogatives at the cost of diverting attention away from the kinds of inquiry and discussion that are most likely to improve the process of learning. This pattern of avoidance probably constitutes one of the reasons why our colleges have not managed to help their students make more impressive gains in such important areas as the capacity to think rigorously or to write with clarity and style.

It is easy to dismiss efforts to improve the process of learning by asserting that education is something that students must obtain for themselves or by insisting that learning is too complex to permit systematic inquiry. Such claims are often self-serving and are almost certainly incorrect, at least in large part. We already understand enough about some elements of the learning process to identify basic steps that can improve education. Other aspects seem susceptible enough to study that serious investigation might bring useful results relatively quickly. Still others may be sufficiently complex to resist examination for years to come. Yet even these topics are probably no more difficult than many subjects to which professors devote entire lifetimes of scholarly inquiry. It is irresponsible not to pay the same serious attention to issues that lie so close to the core of the university's mission. However long it takes, an institution devoted to education must do its best to study the learning process and to assess the effects of its programs. Without such critical self-examination, no human endeavor can possibly make sustained progress.

3

Professional Schools

One of my great distinctions in academic administration was to preside over the Harvard Law School at the time when *The Paper Chase* was written. As the fabled sinner said after being tarred, feathered, and ridden out of town: "If it hadn't been for the honor of it, I'd have just as soon skipped the experience altogether." Outwardly, I displayed no trace of annoyance. Inwardly, I was aggrieved that such a book should have been written. How could a student be ungrateful enough to caricature so grossly the bracing atmosphere of Law School classes?

As time went on, I grew more resigned to reading books about Harvard. I even began to see that they fell into predictable patterns. Most books about undergraduate life, like *Love Story* and *The Last Convertible,* were novels that seemed to surround the College in a warm glow of young love, loud parties, and athletic triumphs. Books about the professional schools were just the opposite. Even novels that spanned the College and a professional school described the two very differently. Readers of *Love Story* will recall that Oliver Barrett IV adored the College and conquered all, but that in the Law School he was turned down flat for financial aid, lived a pinched and penniless existence, and lost his wife to leukemia soon after graduation.

Most books about professional schools are not novels but

long introspective accounts of the first year of study. All are remarkably similar reflections on a youthful enthusiasm battered by the grinding effort to mount the first step toward professional competence. Books such as *One L, Gentle Vengeance,* and *Toughing It Out at Harvard* record a sort of odyssey in which the hero sets forth, filled with hope and apprehension, only to endure a long series of trials and temptations on the way to the shores of some imagined Ithaca. "For all of us who made it through the first year, I am sure that it was a similar undertaking, overwhelming, sometimes frightening, always dizzyingly intense," says Scott Turow, reflecting in *One L* on his experience at law school. With all the worry and struggle, however, when the odyssey has finally ended and the hero emerges, not quite knowing what destination has been reached, Turow, like his companions in medicine and business, acknowledges at last that "everything considered—everything—I would probably do it again."

These troubled accounts cannot obscure the fact that the professional schools in our leading universities are among the finest products of our system of higher education. They are sought after by the ablest graduating seniors in colleges across the country. They attract applicants from nations around the world. They supply the knowledge that gives professions their claim to special competence. With their accomplishments, not surprisingly, come high expectations from outsiders as well as from students. Criticisms are quick to arrive if these expectations are not met. When Chief Justice Burger castigates the bar for failing to achieve high enough standards in the courtroom, he blames the law schools for failing to do a better job. When American corporations falter in competing with the Japanese, *Time* magazine condemns the business schools for overemphasizing the bottom line and underemphasizing long-term productivity and performance. When doctors commit fraud, columnists point to the cutthroat competition to enter medical school and accuse the faculty of failing to instill proper ethical standards in their students.

Such charges are often overdrawn, ignoring other vital influences such as qualities of character or the institutions and social contexts in which professionals practice their calling. But education undoubtedly helps to shape professional behavior, and we have every reason to scrutinize it carefully. How well, then, do professional schools serve the needs of the public? How effective are they in preparing their students for the problems of practice? How quickly do they adapt to changing needs?

There are no simple answers to these questions, for professional schools serve many different callings and come in many sizes and shapes. For example, schools of public health often resemble research institutes rather than educational institutions, whereas schools of architecture tend to do little research and concentrate instead on training students. Schools of education and divinity often ask their students to undergo periods of supervised practice, whereas most schools of public administration offer no experience of this kind. Medical schools have large teaching hospitals in which to train their students, while business schools have nothing that resembles a "teaching corporation." These variations make generalizations difficult. Nevertheless, I believe that we can make some headway by concentrating on the schools that prepare students for the three most powerful and prominent professions: law, business, and medicine.[1]

The Interested Parties

Professional schools are influenced by the expectations and demands of several important audiences: the academy, the students, the profession, and the larger society. These groups share certain premises about professional education. All of them would acknowledge that society must have competent practitioners trained to serve the needs of clients, employers, and the public.

1. Rather than engage in a long discussion over the proper meaning of "profession" and "professional school," let me admit to using these terms loosely to include business and business schools even though one could legitimately describe business as a vocation.

All of them recognize the need for producing new knowledge to enlighten practice. Beneath the agreement on these general principles, however, lurk differences in emphasis and perspective.

The Academy

Every professor who teaches in a school of law, business, or medicine belongs to a community of scholars that includes not only other faculties in the university but other professors in other educational institutions as well. Like the members of any professional body, these scholars share certain values, priorities, ways of defining excellence and status.

High among these values is the importance attached to intellectual achievement. Professors may appreciate the administrative talents of a dean or provost who helps solve their problems and facilitate their work. They may secretly envy colleagues who gain influential posts in government. But they reserve their greatest admiration for those who demonstrate exceptional powers of intellect in making new discoveries, devising new theories, or adding to knowledge in important ways.

Among the many forms of intellectual labor, scholars attach a special value to inquiry that is abstract, theoretical, or interesting for its own sake. They typically assign a lesser status to matters that have immediate, practical utility. To the academic mind, isolating a gene is more important than discovering a better anesthetic for patients; a new conceptual framework for analyzing justice is worth more than a practical suggestion for relieving the congestion of our courts; a novel theory to explain the growth of corporations in the nineteenth century is more significant than a cogently argued plan for competing more effectively with the Japanese.

From these beliefs about the life of the mind comes a tendency to value research over teaching. The reason for this preference is not immediately obvious, since teaching is a demanding activity of central importance to the faculty's mission. But research represents the ultimate expression of a scholar's powers, intellectual labor brought to its highest, most exalted state. Teaching, in contrast, frequently repeats known facts or rehearses the work of others. Even when it breaks new ground, it is often tentative and exploratory in nature, since the new discoveries are not yet committed to the world in irrevocable form. More important, teaching cannot readily be evaluated even by colleagues in one's own institution, let alone by peers in other universities. As a result, published research emerges as the common currency of academic achievement, a currency that can be weighed and evaluated across institutional and even national boundaries. It is, therefore, the chief determinant of status within the guild.

When professors turn to teaching, they are usually inclined to favor theory-building, generalization, and creative insight over the transmission of practical skills. Skills are of great importance to professional practice, as anyone who has undergone major surgery will testify. To teach them well may call for ingenuity of the highest order. But they are rarely the stuff of which academic reputations are made. For one thing, unlike other forms of instruction, the transmission of skills can rarely be translated into important scholarship. For another, such competencies typically call for physical dexterity, psychological awareness, or other talents that are not purely intellectual. Alfred North Whitehead once remarked that the kind of intelligence needed to *perform* professional skills might actually destroy the kind required to *direct* the exercise of skills. If one form of intellect had to go, it was clear which one Whitehead was prepared to sacrifice.

The priorities just discussed are rarely imposed on a professional school faculty by fiat. They impress themselves in other, less obvious ways. They animate the awarding of prizes and other marks of distinction; they creep into conversations and collegial deliberations; they establish themselves in all the subtle ways by which communities confer status and establish hierarchy. Few faculty members in professional schools have the confidence to ignore the rest of the university. Many feel secretly unsure of their status in the shadow of the faculty of arts and sciences—long considered to be the heart of the university where the truest scholars reside. Hence, those who inhabit the professional faculties are concerned not to be dismissed as trade school teachers and anxious to gain the good opinion of their colleagues elsewhere in the institution. To do so, they must manifest a respect for the regnant scholarly values.

The Profession

Medicine, law, and business are all important callings that enjoy ample remuneration and prestige. Their very status has helped to give strength and continuity to the teaching programs of their respective professional schools. Anyone seeking evidence of this phenomenon need simply note the stability in aim and method of the curricula for each of these callings and compare it with the vacillation and uncertainty that have marked the training for more precarious professions such as public administration, education, public health, and social work.

Practicing doctors, lawyers, and executives tend to have priorities quite different from those of the academy. As one might expect, they do not elevate abstract, theoretical ideas over findings of a more practical nature. If anything, the reverse is true. While professionals in all three fields support research that helps improve the quality of practice, lawyers and business executives often grumble about the irrelevance of the more abstract forms of scholarship, and doctors would do the same had basic scientific discoveries not proved their practical worth to medicine so often and so spectacularly. Practitioners also consider teaching to be at least as important as research and probably more so. Although they will accept the need for some historical and theoretical understanding, they favor attempts to teach the basic skills and habits of mind directly relevant to practice. They also support efforts to awaken in students a concern for professional ethics and an interest in the social responsibilities of their calling.

All three professions have ways of bringing their priorities to the attention of their respective schools. Practitioners take a keen interest in their professional schools and give them significant amounts of financial support. The legal and medical professions can bring influence to bear through their power to accredit schools and help set examinations to certify graduates for practice. In theory, at least, practitioners who control corporations, law firms, hospitals, and medical organizations can all exert pressure on professional schools indirectly through their ability to choose which graduates to hire. As spokesmen for their profession, prominent practitioners can also criticize professional education in speeches and articles and other forums. Together, these methods of communication work well enough to bring the views of the profession to the attention of deans and many members of their faculties.

The Students

Students also exert an influence on professional training. By the time they arrive at graduate school, they are seasoned consumers of higher education. They naturally want professors who teach well enough to hold their interest and excite their enthusiasm. They have a strong interest in encouraging the faculty to offer an effective preparation for practice. To this extent, their desires parallel those of the profession. In one respect, however, students' preferences diverge from those of most practitioners. Few students display much interest in studying problems of ethics or issues relating to the responsibilities of the profession. They may arrive at professional school with such concerns. At an early point in their studies, however, they often grow preoccupied with becoming competent practitioners and worried that they will somehow fail in the attempt. Moral dilemmas and social responsibilities come to seem secondary in comparison with the overriding need to master the knowledge and skills required to pass examinations and to cope with the characteristic problems of practice.

Like practitioners, students have various means by which to bring their wishes to the attention of the faculty. They can vote with their feet by deciding which school to attend and what courses to take. In most schools, they can express their satisfactions and displeasures with the quality of teaching by engaging in periodic evaluations of their instructors. Even their responses in class, their flagging interest, their silent disapproval, can have a telling effect on the behavior of the faculty.

The Society

The public has several reasons for being interested in the professions. It needs competent practitioners in sufficient numbers to offer services at reasonable cost to all who seek them. It asks for professionals with high ethical standards who are honest and fair toward their clients and customers and properly sensitive to their needs. In pursuing these interests, the public can do little to influence professional schools directly. Rather, the force of popular opinion resides in its power to rouse to action other agencies, such as newspapers, magazines, foundations, and the government.

These agencies have a wide variety of methods for influencing professional faculties. The media can expose and criticize and thus confront universities with the threat of official intervention. In the 1980s, for example, a wave of hostile publicity caused medical faculties to develop more stringent procedures to deal with scientific fraud. Foundations can offer attractive grants to induce faculties to launch new programs in the public interest. Thus, in the late 1960s the Ford Foundation did much to persuade professional schools to pay more attention to recruiting minority students. On occasion, foundations have even funded elaborate studies of professional education that have helped to bring about significant reform. The Flexner report of 1910 on medical education was an early example, and the Carnegie and Ford Foundation studies on business education, published in 1958, were also influential.

Not surprisingly, the outside agency with the greatest leverage is the government. At the state level, a legislature can influence the size and shape of professional schools in public universities by its decisions in appropriating funds. At the federal level, Washington can distribute money to encourage growth and new activity, as it has done for medical schools by massively funding research. To achieve some compelling national purpose, government officials can even issue rules to limit faculty decisions, as Congress did when it prohibited discrimination on the basis of age, sex, race, religion, or national origin in admitting students or hiring professors.

Although the powers of these groups are varied and formidable, they are rarely used to regulate instruction or curricula in any direct fashion. Since no one has yet found a way to improve teaching by issuing orders to instructors, an outside body cannot accomplish much by trying to dictate the course requirements or the teaching methods professors employ.[2] The closest outsiders normally come to trying to influence such matters occurs when they offer funds to encourage new methods of teaching or to subsidize the training of more doctors, more Ph.D.'s, or more members of some other category of professionals deemed in short supply.

In sum, professional school faculties retain substantial control over the content and the methods of education, but feel significant pressure from their several constituencies in exercising this power. Professors experience conflicting appeals that tug at different sentiments most of them cherish. Students appeal to the instructor's desire to teach well and gain respect in return; the academy and its values evoke the scholar's desire for recognition and prestige; the profession reminds the faculty of the need to prepare students adequately for their chosen calling.

Faculties must also take account of other factors that help determine the content and progress of professional education. Financial or intellectual obstacles frequently prevent even the

2. In medicine, professional groups do influence the curriculum by requiring students to pass national exams, and specialty boards go even further by prescribing the length and much of the content of graduate medical education. At the same time, the content of these requirements is much influenced by professors acting as members of their professional associations. In law, some schools shape their curricula to teach students to pass their bar examinations, but this is not true of the more selective, national law schools situated in research universities.

most conscientious group of professors from providing the kind of instruction desired by students, practitioners, or the public. For example, few schools can afford extensive tutorials, however valuable or popular they may be. Occasionally, adequate technology is not available to make a new teaching method work effectively. Some subjects are so complex that faculty members may not understand them well enough to teach anything worth knowing. Some subjects are so new that it is difficult to find professors who are suitably trained to teach them.

The progress of professional education, then, is largely a result of the interplay of several kinds of pressures and constraints: the claims made by the several interested constituencies, the material and intellectual factors that limit what is possible in the classroom, and the habits and attitudes ingrained within the faculty. The interaction of these forces reveals itself most vividly when faculties confront certain strategic questions common to every professional school.

Balancing Teaching and Research

As with all demanding activities, the quality of teaching varies according to the effort that instructors devote to it. This obvious truth becomes a critical issue in a university where professors have many competing demands on their time—to teach, to publish, to administer and to advise.

We have already seen how practitioners and the academy differ on the importance of teaching and research. Faculty members are caught between these conflicting expectations. In striking a balance, different schools arrive at different solutions. Medical faculties are plainly oriented toward research, and most of their professors have teaching loads that seem puny to their colleagues in law and business schools. They care much less about the quality of their instruction than about their progress in the laboratory, where the rewards of professional recognition and status are chiefly to be found. In contrast, law schools put much more emphasis on the quality of teaching. Even the law faculties most renowned for their scholarship have traditionally attached as much importance to instruction as they have to research, and their ranks have typically included a significant number of professors who have published relatively little.

What accounts for this difference? One reason, surely, is the vital role of medical research in improving human health. In view of the critical importance the public places on conquering disease, Congress appropriates billions of dollars each year for this purpose. Since government research grants carry with them funds to help pay for library costs, building maintenance, and other fixed expenses, the university itself develops a keen interest in having a faculty that can attract such grants. Small wonder, then, that medical schools place a higher priority on research than do faculties of law. Law professors, after all, receive almost no government support for research, and the public has little interest in a process of inquiry that never announces dramatic solutions to deeply felt human problems. Even the practicing bar is only moderately concerned with legal scholarship and has little or no interest in the more theoretical work that has increasingly caught the fancy of professors in recent years.

Yet money and public attention cannot fully explain the relative importance of teaching and research. Business school professors do not attract nearly as much outside funding as that enjoyed by their medical colleagues, and their research has not even had the impact on the practice of management that law faculties have exerted on legal rules and procedures. Nevertheless, most leading business schools emphasize research over teaching and look more to publications than to the quality of instruction in deciding which young faculty members to promote.

These patterns of behavior reveal another factor that helps to explain how different faculties strike a balance between teaching and research. All professional schools must decide whether to choose their professors primarily from their own graduates or from discipline-oriented Ph.D. programs. This is no insignificant decision. The choice that a school makes does much to determine its style and its priorities.

Faculty members recruited from the profession are more likely to place a high value on teaching. When they publish, their writings usually relate to problems of interest to the practitioner, especially if they themselves have practiced for a substantial period. Conversely, professors recruited from Ph.D. programs are generally drawn to research rather than teaching, since research is what is stressed most heavily in doctoral training. In keeping with the values of the departments where they received their degrees, they are inclined to explore problems for their own intrinsic interest rather than to search for ideas that will help practitioners perform better (though the two types of inquiry sometimes coincide). They tend to teach by lecturing rather than by conducting discussions about problems culled from practice. In addition, able Ph.D.'s rarely wish to work in isolation. They usually insist on having colleagues from the same discipline with whom to share ideas, graduate students whom they can train, laboratories, computers, or libraries with which to carry out their investigations. All in all, faculty members recruited from Ph.D. programs tend to transform the academic environment in which they serve and to orient it more toward research than toward training practitioners.

The Training of the Faculty

Law schools are perhaps the leading example of professional schools that have chosen to rely on their own graduates rather than on Ph.D.'s to staff the faculty. Economists, political scientists, and sociologists have always been thought to lack sufficient knowledge of legal doctrine, legal institutions, and the methods of legal reasoning to teach students "how to think like a lawyer." Of course, this policy could not work if the ablest students insisted on forsaking the academy for the riches to be won in legal practice. Fortunately, law faculties have always been able to attract many of their very best graduates to a life of teaching—presumably because law schools have traditionally enrolled many able students who enter with no real commitment to practice.

The decision to recruit faculty in this manner is not without cost. Law graduates are well prepared to train students in rigorous doctrinal reasoning and in critical analyses of court opinions. With rare exceptions, however, they did not enter law school intending a career in research. They have no training in a scholarly discipline and know nothing of the more sophisticated methods of quantitative or empirical investigation. As a result, our understanding of how the legal system actually works and what effects it has on those it purports to serve has not advanced nearly as much as it might have done if law schools had chosen to recruit more Ph.D.'s to their faculties.

Business schools have consciously chosen a different path. In contrast to law faculties, they have found it very difficult to persuade their best graduates to enter an academic career. Instead, they have turned increasingly to economists and other Ph.D.'s and encouraged them to learn enough about business to teach their students effectively. With the influx of Ph.D.'s, these schools have also come to be noted for research of a kind that demands the specialized training and techniques possessed only by those graduating from faculties of arts and sciences or their equivalent. Unlike traditional legal scholarship, much of this research is quite sophisticated and abstract and has little immediate application to the practical problems of business. As such, it provokes periodic complaints from exasperated executives and other critics. This carping has but slight effect on faculties composed of Ph.D.'s, who have little affinity with the practicing manager but a deep respect for the norms of scholarship imposed by the scholarly disciplines through their learned journals.

At times, a professional school will seek to find a middle course that avoids the dilemma of having to opt for a faculty of Ph.D.'s interested in research or one composed primarily of its own graduates who lack advanced research skills. For example, many law schools have hired a philosopher, an economist, or even a psychologist to examine legal questions from a different perspective. More recently, such schools have also been able to recruit law graduates who have taken advanced work in one of the social science disciplines. Appointments of this kind are increasingly tempting as legal scholars perceive important connections to more and more fields of knowledge. Yet these strategies are hardly ideal. Since law schools are unwilling to hire large numbers of Ph.D.'s or to commit substantial resources to graduate training or research, the environment is rarely tempting enough to attract truly outstanding scholars from other disciplines.[3] At the same time, law graduates who have taken advanced work in other fields are rarely expert enough to do first-rate discipline-based research. The danger, then, is that scholarship will fall between two stools, neither practical enough to aid in the rational development of legal rules nor powerful enough to make a lasting contribution to theory.

Another strategy, employed by a few business faculties, has been to hire young Ph.D.'s and encourage them to learn the ways of the professional school, with its emphasis on the practical problems of the profession and on Socratic methods of teaching. This effort may succeed, but it also carries high risks. Some of the recruits will not adapt to the demands of Socratic teaching; others adapt so well that they cease to do research of any lasting, fundamental importance. Worse yet, the better Ph.D.'s may be unwilling to come at all on such terms. Unless they are virtually assured of tenure from the start, they know that they may face an agonizing choice. Either they can accept the ways of the professional school and burn their bridges back to the discipline or they can try to do the kind of scholarly work that will keep their disciplinary credentials in order and thereby compromise their chances for internal promotion. Faced with such a choice, if the research that the faculty requires differs sharply from accepted forms of scholarship in the discipline, an able Ph.D. is likely to shun the business school altogether.

3. Some of the smaller professional schools, such as those in public administration, education, and architecture, have managed to attract excellent scholars, especially by giving them joint appointments with their parent departments in arts and sciences. Such examples are few, however, and carry a constant risk that the scholars involved will drift away from the professional schools and gradually move back to their departments.

Thus a professional school will often find itself with an awkward choice. By hiring Ph.D.'s, it can press for scholarly distinction at the risk of distancing itself from the profession and from teaching about its practical problems. By hiring its own graduates, it can emphasize good teaching and study issues relevant to practice at the expense of research that only trained investigators can perform—sophisticated laboratory science, elaborate empirical investigation, or quantitative and computer-aided inquiry.

The one sure way to avoid this dilemma is to be large enough and wealthy enough to accommodate both types of professors in considerable numbers. Few faculties other than medical schools can afford this strategy. With the help of massive research support from the government and ample revenue derived from patient fees, medical faculties can hire basic scientists to work in fields such as biochemistry and cell biology as well as clinicians to do applied research of immediate relevance to patient care. To be sure, medical schools succeed with this strategy only at the risk of separating their faculty into two distinct cultures, which often clash with each other over money and space. Still, they have proven that with sufficient funds a faculty can have the best of both worlds, providing teaching and research of a basic *and* a practical nature.

What to Teach?

All faculties of law, medicine, and business seek to convey to their students a systematic way of thinking about the characteristic problems of their profession. Law schools call this "learning to think like a lawyer." Harvard Business School speaks of inculcating "the administrative point of view." Medical students develop such habits of thought in courses with titles like "Introduction to the Clinic" and continue to hone them during repeated rounds through the hospital wards. This way of thinking is what law professors instill through the Socratic method and what business school faculty members convey through the discussion of problems and the use of computer games. It represents a sort of paradigm of the professional mind in action.

All of these paradigmatic modes of thought demand a store of relevant information, a mastery of particular skills, and an ability to analyze complex problems, but the different professional schools vary in the relative emphasis placed on these three forms of mental activity. The differences emerge most clearly in the response that schools of law, business, and medicine have made to a problem that has faced them all: how to cope with the rising flood of relevant knowledge.

In the early years of professional education, all faculties emphasized the transmission of useful information. Law professors discoursed on the statutes and judicial opinions that set forth the prevailing legal rules. Business school professors taught survey courses on railroads, public utilities, retailing, and the like. Medical school professors lectured on the human body and its biological processes.

As time went on, faculties found it increasingly difficult to teach in this fashion. The volume of relevant information became so vast that students could not remember more than a fraction of what they learned. Moreover, in rapidly changing fields, facts that seemed important when first taught often grew obsolete or irrelevant after a few years.

These problems first became acute for law schools in the latter part of the nineteenth century, as industrialization wrought great changes in legal doctrine and as laws began to diverge more and more from one state to another. If students did not know in what state they would practice, faculties could not choose which body of law to teach them; and of course it was impossible to anticipate the changes in legal doctrine that would occur within their lifetimes. The remedy came, perhaps inadvertently, through the introduction of the case method. This technique consisted of having students read the opinions of judges in actual cases and then discuss the opinions in class to analyze the judges' reasoning and apply it to slightly different situations. The critical insight in this method was the recognition that students did not need to memorize rules; they could always look them up later on when the occasion arose in their practice. What students had to learn was how to *use* rules and how to analyze them rigorously enough to be able to apply them in novel situations. As the new form of teaching took hold, students still learned much about legal doctrine, institutions, and procedures, but facts and information were clearly subordinated to method. What mattered most was the ability to reason systematically.

Business schools, which were founded much later than law schools, also began by giving descriptive courses: either about mining, utilities, and other sectors of the economy or about business methods, such as budgeting or accounting. But professors soon found that the workings of the economy and the affairs of corporate enterprise were too complex for all the relevant information to be compressed into lectures and readings. Faced with this problem, Harvard Business School, later joined by other schools, instituted policies similar to those followed by the law faculties. Professors began to write "cases" based on business problems adapted from real life. Instead of lecturing, instructors discussed these cases with students in class. Courses were no longer arranged according to sectors of the economy but were grouped by separate functions common to almost all business enterprises—production, personnel, marketing, and the like. Once again, the emphasis shifted from transmitting information to teaching critical thinking. The aim was to train students to perceive problems, analyze them carefully, and then make decisions as a manager would do in a real corporation.

In contrast to their counterparts in the law, however, business faculties did not all take to the case method as the dominant form of instruction. Another group of schools organized themselves by disciplines and subdisciplines, such as finance, macroeconomics, and statistics. These faculties also emphasized decisionmaking, but their instructors chose to spend much less time discussing business problems. Instead they lectured to their classes in a manner reminiscent of a college or a graduate school of arts and sciences. Still, the essential point is that business schools, like law faculties, eventually found it necessary to subordinate the task of conveying information to the teaching of analytic technique. This tendency was just as true of schools emphasizing a discipline-based curriculum as it was of faculties that taught by the case method.[4]

Medical schools, interestingly, have still not given up the effort to transmit large quantities of information to students through lectures. Although students eventually learn practical skills and methods of analysis in their years of supervised work in teaching hospitals, they pass their first two years listening to lectures and assimilating formidable amounts of detailed scientific data. The feats of memory required of these students have long been legendary. With the discovery of the structure of DNA, the volume of scientific information that students learn has now grown so vast that medical education is under severe strain. As one waggish survivor once described it, the first year of medical school is akin to memorizing the entire Manhattan telephone book—backward.

Two or three small medical schools—notably the University of New Mexico and McMaster University in Canada—have already broken away from the dominant tradition to develop a problem-based curriculum featuring small groups and active discussion. Although the larger schools have been slow to follow suit, Harvard has now introduced a radically new pilot program following proposals recently made by a blue-ribbon panel of experts convened by the Association of American Medical Colleges. For the most part, however, the traditional pattern continues.

4. Both case-method schools and discipline-oriented schools still exist (though most faculties now try to blend the two approaches to some extent). Each type has its ardent supporters. In the end, the persistence of two different methods may have less to do with the merits of the respective approaches than with differences of a more practical sort. During their formative years, schools whose faculties were composed primarily of Ph.D.'s tended to adopt a discipline-based approach emphasizing lectures, while the case method found favor in schools whose faculties were more heavily populated by business school graduates. As time went on, another factor proved important. Faculties had to spend so much time and money going out into the field to produce good cases that fewer and fewer schools could afford to continue teaching by this method. By now, the cost of producing cases is sufficiently high that few schools other than Harvard can afford to create such material in significant quantity.

It is tempting to conclude that medical schools are simply behind the times and that their research-oriented faculties are unwilling to make the effort to revise the curricula and master a different method of teaching. This indeed may be the proper explanation. But it is just possible that doctors, in contrast to lawyers or business executives, need to command greater quantities of information in order to conduct a physical examination, think of the many possible hypotheses to account for the patient's symptoms, and order the right tests, interpret the results, and eventually arrive at a valid diagnosis. It is said that great chess masters are people who keep in their heads an enormous number of prior games, which they can use to decide what to do in any situation they encounter. Conceivably, doctors work in much the same way.

Yet even if doctors must carry around vast amounts of information, the burdens on medical students have become so heavy that leading spokesmen for the medical establishment have begun to express acute concern. Hence, the prospects for change seem brighter than ever before. In all probability, medical schools of the future will expect students to remember less detail during their first two years. Much of what they do have to absorb will be learned more efficiently with the help of programmed instruction. With fewer lectures and less memorization, students will spend more time learning how to find relevant information (with the help of the computer), how to make complex judgments (using statistics and other decisionmaking techniques), and how to analyze problems (through the discussion of cases in small groups). If medical schools move in these directions, emphasizing methods of reasoning over memorization, they will be following belatedly along the path taken earlier by faculties of law and business.

What Is Left Out?

I have already noted that all professional schools seek not only to transmit information but to develop in each student a disciplined way of thinking about the characteristic problems of practice. This paradigmatic mode of thought features what professional faculties teach best: careful analysis fortified by specialized knowledge and technique. Congenial to professors and central to the work that professionals do, the paradigm occupies a dominant place in the teaching and thinking of the faculty. Invariably, however, it omits certain subject matter that is widely considered vital to practice. Hence, the preoccupation with one form of analysis provokes complaints from working professionals who see important aspects of their work being ignored.

Practical Skills

Much of what is left out consists of practical, everyday skills. Judges and attorneys often assert that law schools fail to teach their students how to draft a will, interview a witness, or enter a timely objection to testimony in a trial. Executives point out that new M.B.A.'s cannot even write adequately, let alone bargain with a union leader. Doctors are less inclined to make such claims, since medical students spend years practicing in hospitals as interns and residents after completing their basic studies. Even so, they rarely learn the statistical techniques required to deal adequately with complex decisions using intricate bodies of data. Moreover, experienced physicians often complain that students see only the most exotic, complicated cases in teaching hospitals and spend little time learning how to treat the simpler ailments they will often encounter in private practice.

Prominent among the competencies that do not get much emphasis from professional faculties are the skills of human relations. In a recent survey of 1,600 attorneys who graduated from law school between 1955 and 1970, 69 percent said that they had not been trained to counsel with clients, and 77 percent declared that law school had not prepared them adequately to negotiate a settlement. Corporate executives likewise insist that the most important skills are the ones they never learned as students: leading and motivating subordinates and working effectively with peers. In medicine, over one-third of those who visit a doctor have only a psychosomatic ailment, most patients do not give their physicians a complete and accurate medical history, 30 percent do not follow instructions for medication and treatment, and many diseases could be avoided if doctors could persuade their patients to change their personal habits. In the face of such evidence, it is critically important for doctors to understand human psychology and to learn how to communicate effectively with patients. Yet most medical students receive no systematic instruction in matters of this kind.

Prominent practitioners complain periodically about the failure of professional schools to teach these human and practical skills. Until the last ten or fifteen years, however, the complaints were infrequent and their impact was minimal. Often, such charges went unanswered. If the critic was sufficiently well known, a dean or a prominent professor would reply, but rarely sympathetically. The usual response was to dismiss the complaints as anti-intellectual or to argue that ordinary skills should be learned in practice, where students could pick them up through actual experience.

Examining this record, a cynic might conclude that professional school faculties have failed to teach these skills simply because they prefer not to and feel no effective pressure to do so. But more substantial causes are also at work. For one thing, important skills may be hard to teach because professors may not understand them well enough to be able to construct generalizations, insights, or conceptual frameworks worth communicating. Leadership is a case in point. Everyone acknowledges its importance, but few are confident that they can define its vital ingredients, let alone teach them to a class. Other skills, such as legal drafting, seem so mechanical and dull that instructors avoid teaching them for fear of boring their students.

Notwithstanding these problems, there are probably very few competencies that are impossible to teach effectively. Eventually, some professor will succeed in understanding almost every skill well enough to create a useful, stimulating course. Progress of this kind does occur, albeit slowly. For example, law schools learned in the 1960s how to teach effective courses in trial practice, and there are promising signs that classes in mediation and negotiation may now be feasible as well. Business schools are able to offer useful work in collective bargaining and human relations. More and more medical schools are offering courses on the social dimensions of illness. Many schools of management are experimenting with teaching such intangibles as leadership skills and entrepreneurship. Faculty members in schools of law and medicine are trying new ways to teach interviewing and counseling. Many of these initiatives use videotape, computers, simulation exercises, and other innovative methods to improve the quality of learning.

The key question, then, is not whether improvement can occur, but at what pace the process of experimentation will proceed. Experience suggests that the rate of progress depends not only on the ingenuity of professors but also on the needs that arise in the outside world and on the intensity of criticism from practitioners and students. A good example of this phenomenon has occurred in most leading law schools during the last fifteen years.

Although practitioners have always grumbled about the "ivory tower" approach of most law faculties, complaints from bench and bar about the competence of lawyers suddenly intensified in the early 1970s. Speaking in 1973, Chief Justice Burger announced the "working hypothesis that from one-third to one-half of the lawyers who appear [in court] in the serious cases are not really qualified."[5] A committee appointed by an influential federal judge responded to this attack and other similar charges by issuing strong recommendations for compulsory training in trial advocacy and related courses.[6] Surveys of practicing attorneys gave further ammunition to critics by revealing

5. Warren E. Burger, "The Special Skills of Advocacy: Are Specialized Training and Certification of Advocates Essential to Our System of Justice?" *Fordham Law Review* 42 (1973): 234.

6. "Qualifications for Practice before the United States Courts in the Second Circuit: Final Report of the Advisory Committee on Proposed Rules for Admission to Practice," *Federal Rules Decisions* 67 (1976): 159.

that few respondents believed their legal education had prepared them to use skills essential to their profession.

At about the same time these attacks were being made, an innovation occurred in many law schools. Clinics were established that allowed law students to represent poor people in cases of divorce, eviction, discrimination, and other common legal disputes. Such programs multiplied during the next ten years, quickly extending to the vast majority of law schools. They offered a way to train students in practical skills while supplying needy clients with important services. In contrast with the largely unsupervised legal aid programs of earlier years, the newer clinics engaged experienced instructors to work with students and help them learn to gather facts, interview witnesses, draft pleadings, and plan litigation. As time went on, some of the teachers involved in this work began using simulation techniques to provide skills training more systematically and at a lower cost. Other faculty members started to teach additional skills, such as negotiation and mediation, with the help of simulations and role-playing. Before long, students were receiving instruction in a variety of skills that had not been previously taught to any significant extent. The amount of experimentation vastly exceeded anything seen in law schools during the preceding thirty years.

Expressions of concern from the profession were undoubtedly one impetus for this innovative effort, but they were by no means the only one. The student activism of the late 1960s certainly played a role. Support from the Ford Foundation, and later the War on Poverty, also helped to persuade many schools that they could afford to move ahead. Clinical programs won further favor in the eyes of law school deans because they seemed to offer a way of breathing life into the last two years of legal training by giving students a chance to learn new skills while actually working on "live" cases of their own.

These favoring forces were enough to get clinical programs started at a rapid clip. As time went on, however, the programs began to encounter obstacles that kept them from being integrated securely into the center of the law school. For one thing, they were much more expensive than regular instruction, since effective supervision demanded much lower student-faculty ratios than were needed for traditional instruction. In addition, faculty members in the clinical programs were different from the typical professor. They worked intensively with students while carrying heavy caseloads and hence had little time for research. Their talents tended to lie in litigating rather than in writing articles. In unguarded moments, they sometimes revealed a disdain for their more traditional colleagues for failing to understand the real world and for devoting their talents to preparing students to work in establishment law firms.

Misunderstandings quickly developed. Clinical instructors felt that they were not sufficiently appreciated and were treated as second-class citizens. Regular faculty members believed that full faculty appointments should go only to members who did distinguished research. As tensions grew, traditional professors began to wonder whether clinical programs were really worth the price and whether the skills they imparted might be better left to be learned in practice or taught by classroom simulations at much lower cost.

Amid these conflicting opinions, the future of the new programs remains uncertain. Many faculty members still support them because they are popular with students and because they supply needed services to the poor. At the same time, their funding is often inadequate, and the career prospects offered to clinical instructors seem too problematic to attract the ablest people. Conceivably, the clinics might develop—as they have in medical schools—into a separate but equal part of the school with faculty members chosen for their special talents. But this path would require resources not yet in sight and a supply of able faculty not yet available. For the time being, clinical programs remain in limbo, an experiment whose ultimate success is still in doubt. As with so many recent innovations in the teaching of new skills, some enterprising professors have made a promising start, but the resulting programs have not yet been integrated into the core of the curriculum where they will be taken by large majorities of students.

Ethics and Social Responsibility

In none of the three types of professional schools did the traditional curriculum attach much importance to courses on the ethical problems of practice or the social responsibilities of the profession. Leading practitioners and prominent figures periodically called upon faculties to pay more attention to these subjects. Surveys of the professions regularly recorded the belief of most practitioners that such topics, especially ethics, deserved greater emphasis. And yet, for generations, faculties did not respond.

Why professional schools should have avoided these subjects is not immediately clear. It is not impossible to teach effective classes in professional ethics and social responsibility; excellent models can be readily found in classrooms across the country. But the problem may be harder than it at first appears, for courses in these subjects begin with a considerable handicap. They fall outside the accepted paradigm of professional training and are vulnerable to the charge of being soft and lacking in analytical rigor. A noted law professor, Karl Llewellyn, used to tell his first-year students:

> The hardest job of the first year is to lop off your common sense, to knock your ethics into temporary anaesthesia. Your view of social policy, your sense of justice—to knock these out of your system along with woozy thinking, along with ideas all fuzzed along their edges. You are to acquire the ability to think precisely, to analyze coldly, to work within a body of materials that is given . . .[7]

Llewellyn knew that students needed to reacquire their ethical sensibilities at a later stage, after mastering the basic skills of legal analysis. Presumably, faculty members in business and medicine would agree. Yet students may not quickly recover

7. K. N. Llewellyn, *The Bramble Bush: On Our Law and Its Study* (New York: Oceana, 1960), p. 116.

their interest in ethics. Many of them have an instinctive apprehension that ethics will somehow get in the way of tough-minded, "objective" analysis. As interest mounts over finding jobs and commencing practice, students turn to other things.

Faculties also have difficulty finding qualified professors to teach professional ethics. Such instructors must have an unusual background that includes both a familiarity with moral philosophy and a knowledge of at least one profession. Because the preparation needed cannot be given within any single academic program, such people are hard to find. As a result, professors who offer these courses tend to be less adequately trained and hence less likely to impress colleagues with the value of their subject and the merit of its claim for a respected place within the core of the professional curriculum.

As with the teaching of skills, however, there have been recent signs of a quickening interest in this subject. Curiously enough, the movement first arose in medical schools, even though moral philosophy is further from the educational background of medical professors than from that of their colleagues in law or business. The interest in offering such courses seems to have come about for a combination of reasons. For one thing, as the well-known case of Karen Ann Quinlan revealed, ethical problems in medicine often join with compelling issues of life and death to attract wide public attention. Technological advances, such as *in vitro* fertilization and behavior modification, create other arresting moral questions. The threat of adverse publicity and the growing risk of malpractice litigation make such issues a matter of personal concern to doctors. Against this backdrop, a few philosophers and physicians have managed to prepare themselves to offer courses on the moral dilemmas of practice. As yet, however, such courses do not attract more than a small minority of the students in most medical schools.

Business faculties too have begun introducing courses on the ethical issues confronting executives and the social responsibilities of corporations. As late as 1958, major reports on business education did not even mention ethics in their indexes. By 1972,

40 percent of all business schools offered a course in this subject, and 84 percent did so by 1978. Nevertheless, management faculties have not yet produced able scholars interested in serious research and writing on these topics. A recent study points out that "with a handful of individual exceptions," business school professors "are simply not able to sustain serious theoretical reflection on the ethical dimensions of business activity, even if they were so inclined." As a result, according to the same study, "relatively few business schools offer courses that orient the consideration of economic and management decisions by ethical concepts and topics as criteria for choice."[8]

Much the same is true of courses on the social responsibilities of corporations. Such offerings are now common. Still, few influential voices from our schools of management speak out on issues of corporate responsibility or the role of free enterprise, even though many prominent executives believe that public attitudes about the corporation's place in society will have a decisive influence on the future of American business. Corporate leaders sometimes complain that academic critics have a bias against business, citing authors such as John Kenneth Galbraith, Charles Lindblom, and Robert Heilbroner. Yet the wonder is not that critics of business exist, but that so few members of the leading management faculties are willing or able to contribute significantly to the debate. As with ethics, courses in social responsibility are still peripheral to the interests of most business schools, and there is little sign of a growing body of scholarship strong enough to make such courses more central in the near future.

In law schools, faculties traditionally offered no more than a few sparsely attended courses in ethics and problems of professional responsibility. In the late 1960s, these classes were reinforced by the rapid growth of clinical programs. Some clinics included instruction in problems of ethics, access to legal services, and the social responsibilities of the bar. Some did not.

8. Charles W. Powers and David Vogel, *Ethics in the Education of Business Managers* (New York: Hastings Center, 1980), pp. 58, 36.

But all of them at least exposed their students to these issues in a remarkably vivid way. The act of representing real clients from poor neighborhoods probably did more to raise student consciousness about the adequacy of legal services and the moral dilemmas of practice than did most of the existing courses on the subject.

Shortly after the advent of the clinics, fresh support arrived from a different quarter. For years, spokesmen for the profession had urged law schools to require courses on ethics and social responsibility, but deans had successfully resisted these proposals. In 1973, in the aftermath of Watergate, the American Bar Association and representatives of the law schools finally agreed on a resolution requiring that all students take instruction in professional responsibility as a prerequisite for admission to the bar.

The experience of law schools offers a rare illustration of an attempt to achieve curricular reform through compulsion. The results have been interesting. With the ABA requirement, law graduates are much less likely to enter practice ignorant of important issues of professional ethics and the delivery of legal services. In addition, many professors have had to acquaint themselves with these subjects in order to teach the necessary courses. Still, the fruits of this effort have not been all that leaders of the bar presumably hoped. Surveys evaluating the results of the ABA rule suggest that the resulting courses are usually valued less highly by students and thought to be less interesting, less demanding, and less well taught than the traditional offerings in the curriculum. As for research, much more work than before is undoubtedly going on in such fields as alternative dispute settlement and legal services for the poor. But the corpus of serious writing on the ethical problems of practice is still small, and few professors look upon the subject as their major field of interest. Moreover, research on the problems of the legal system and of access to legal services continues to be hampered by the fact that law professors are seldom trained for empirical investigation and hence cannot carry on much of the work that is most needed in these fields.

The ABA requirement seems to have acted as a catalyst to encourage greater faculty involvement in teaching legal ethics and professional responsibility. But involvement by fiat does not guarantee success. Unless compulsion can ignite a genuine interest within the faculty and a willingness on the part of some professors to specialize in the subject, the gains will continue to be limited. On this score, as far as law schools are concerned, the jury is still out.

Evaluating Our Professional Schools

With this brief account of the forces that shape professional education, it is time to step back and ask how well the system works. Do faculties respond adequately to the needs of their students? Do these students receive training good enough to enable them to give competent service? Are they prepared to be leaders in their profession and to serve the public interest by working to improve the standards and performance of their calling?

Judgments about the quality of professional training are largely subjective, for efforts to measure the impact of education at this level are even more meager and unsatisfactory than research on undergraduate education. Nevertheless, scraps of available evidence should give us satisfaction, at least in comparing our methods of professional education with those of other countries. Although the evidence is impressionistic, our doctors seem to be as well prepared as those of any country in the world. A few countries, such as Great Britain, may do a better job of preparing effective general practitioners, thus helping to meet the full gamut of national health needs. But no nation can surpass the United States in the quality of preparation for more specialized, sophisticated branches of medicine. The desire of outstanding young physicians around the globe to come to America for advanced training helps confirm that assessment. In contrast, reports from abroad suggest that many medical schools in Europe suffer from one or more of the same problems that afflict their parent universities: overcrowding and overenrollment, politicized governance, excessive centralization and regulation.

American business schools also attract many students from abroad and have been emulated widely in Europe and parts of the Third World. More and more foreign students seem to be either seeking admission to management programs in this country or enrolling in institutions abroad that are heavily influenced by the American model. One can certainly find critics of our methods of management education, notably in Japan, where many large corporations refuse to hire business school graduates, preferring to train their managers themselves. Yet even in Japan the leading school of management, at Keio University, modeled itself explicitly on the Harvard Business School. What is at issue in Japan is not whether there are university programs in business that are superior to ours but whether the very idea of academic training for management is sound.

Legal education is harder to compare internationally, since law studies are so dependent on the particular rules, institutions, and practices of each nation. In contrast to our system, with its emphasis on problem-solving and legal reasoning, legal education in Europe, in the words of John Merryman, "is more abstract, more concerned with questions of philosophic than immediate practical importance, more removed from the solution of social problems."[9] Professors in Europe tend to regard law as a science of sorts to be taught didactically in large lecture courses. Comparative studies also reveal that many fewer instructors abroad are full-time faculty members and that they tend to have little interest in evaluating the education they offer or in considering how to make it better. Foreign law schools are often overcrowded; for example, the Faculty of Law in Rome boasts more than twelve thousand students. In these bloated institutions, few students prepare conscientiously for class or even attend regularly, and most are enrolled only on a part-time basis. Education can scarcely prosper in such circumstances.

9. John Henry Merryman, "Legal Education There and Here: A Comparison," *Stanford Law Review* 27 (1975): 866.

Only in one aspect of legal training do other countries appear to surpass the United States, and that is the systematic effort in many European nations to give all students opportunities to practice under competent supervision. But even this activity is the work of the practicing bar and is not administered by the universities.

Though the better professional schools in this country stand up well under international comparison, our system of professional education is not without faults. Some of the deficiencies result from genuine intellectual problems or barriers of cost. But some do not. In attempting to serve their major constituencies, our schools of law, business, and medicine have not yet succeeded in responding adequately to several important needs.

Student Needs

In all three faculties, professors have long struggled with certain basic dilemmas in teaching their students. The nature of these difficulties differs markedly from one type of school to another. The perennial problem for law schools has been to sustain student interest after the highly successful first year, since most of the courses thereafter, whatever the subject matter, continue to train students in the same basic methods of legal analysis. As one professor put it: "To be mercifully brief, law school is unmercifully dull . . . because the only skill learned after the first year is the skill of feigning preparedness for class."[10] In the more prestigious schools, this problem is compounded by the endless visits of law-firm recruiters who begin at the end of the first year to distract students with offers and negotiations for summer jobs.

Conversely, medical education grows increasingly varied and interesting as time passes. The critical problem arises from the almost total concentration on the biomedical sciences and is most intense in the first two years. During this period, students

10. Thomas F. Bergin, "The Law Teacher: A Man Divided against Himself," *Virginia Law Review* 54 (1968): 648.

endure countless lectures and memorize huge quantities of basic scientific material, much of which they promptly forget. In the words of a recent national report by a distinguished panel of educators: "Medical faculties have thought it imperative that medical education keep pace with biomedical science and have expanded the base of factual knowledge that students must commit to memory. By this concentration on the transmittal of factual information, faculties have neglected to help them acquire the skills, values, and attitudes that are the foundation of a helping profession."[11]

Faculties of business have yet a different problem. In contrast to their colleagues in law and medicine, management professors have not agreed on how to define, let alone how to teach, the essential tasks that corporate executives perform. Lawyers use a disciplined form of reasoning when they analyze legal problems and argue cases; doctors do the same in applying their fund of medical knowledge to diagnose an ailment and prescribe appropriate treatment. What the successful manager actually does in order to be successful, however, is much harder to isolate and teach. Since fewer than 20 percent of the chief executive officers of large corporations have business school degrees (though the figure is rising), there is even a nagging possibility that formal training is unnecessary for effective management. These uncertainties may help to explain why business schools differ among themselves so much more than other professional schools in the content and method of their instruction.

All of these basic dilemmas have endured for a long time. The criticisms one hears from students today seem identical to complaints their predecessors uttered decades ago. Perhaps the perennial quality of these problems merely shows how difficult they are to resolve. Yet one wonders whether faculties have tried hard enough. Surely, much of the recent progress made by law schools in diversifying methods of instruction could have been achieved decades earlier. High-level reports on medical

11. *Physicians for the Twenty-first Century: Report of the Panel on the General Professional Education of the Physician and College Preparation for Medicine* (Washington, D.C.: Association of American Medical Colleges, 1984), pp. 2, 3.

education likewise suggest that faculties could have done much more to integrate basic and clinical science and to cut back the use of lectures had they not been so intent upon research. The continued emphasis in most business schools on discipline-based technique and the tendency to ignore many of the practical problems of management look suspiciously like the path of least resistance for a faculty of Ph.D.'s preoccupied with their scholarly work. In all three types of schools, a sluggish rate of progress betrays the lack of effective pressure for reform.

Professional Needs

Through the years, professional faculties have also failed to do as much as they should to impart basic skills, especially those involving bargaining, counseling, persuasion, and other forms of human interaction. Such competencies have always been essential to practice. Although some of them are difficult to teach, very few are impossible. For generations, however, most faculties never bothered to make a determined effort.

In recent years, there have been unmistakable signs of progress in many schools. Numerous experiments have been tried for teaching a variety of skills. For the most part, however, these offerings are still taught to only a small fraction of the student body by a few dedicated professors. Such instructors deserve great encouragement and support for their accomplishments. Instead, they often remain outside the accepted paradigm of instruction, making less of an impact on the training of students than their potential contribution warrants.

Faculty spokesmen may reply that most skills are safely left to be learned in practice, where students can master them under the eye of experienced professionals. According to this view, formal education should be reserved for the kinds of analysis and conceptual reasoning for which it is uniquely suited. But this is hardly a satisfactory answer. Many beginning practitioners do not work in a setting where they can receive close, competent supervision as they acquire needed skills. More important, the argument misconceives the proper relationship between academic learning and experience. Formal instruction and practice should not be viewed as alternatives; they are complementary, in the sense that neither works optimally without the other. What the university can do is to teach students to analyze different skills, understand their constituent elements, and comprehend how the elements function to achieve a desired result. In this way, formal instruction enables students to reflect more fruitfully on their later experience and, through such reflection, to arrive at a higher level of proficiency.

Presumably, faculties would work harder to teach professional skills if students or employers exerted greater pressure on them to do so. Only rarely does pressure of this kind materialize. The most influential employers are the larger organizations, which can most readily take it on themselves to teach the necessary skills on the job. As for students, very few know enough to question faculty judgments on what to teach. The result is not that professors cavalierly ignore the needs of the profession; they hear the complaints from practitioners and acknowledge their responsibility to prepare students well. But a sense of urgency is lacking. In an environment where each professor can decide what to teach and little prestige attaches to the teaching of skills, progress tends to be much slower than it would be if the welfare of the institution depended on making improvements rapidly.

Public Needs

Society expects a great deal from the professions, especially the three I have been discussing. Though legal proceedings are often frustrating, only in Shakespeare does anyone really want to kill all the lawyers. Everyone else understands, albeit grudgingly, that the nation does need attorneys—as well as corporate executives and physicians. The trick is to prepare trained people in the right numbers to fill society's requirements. No country seems able to achieve this goal consistently. In the United States, shortages have occasionally occurred. More often, gluts have appeared, most recently of Ph.D.'s and increasingly of doctors as well. Indeed, although America seems to have an almost limitless capacity to absorb lawyers, newspapers have even begun to mention a surfeit of attorneys.

Surpluses have emerged partly because professional education is often heavily subsidized and partly because students are sometimes too optimistic in estimating their chances for success in a bleak market. As I have already pointed out, however, centrally planned systems are just as erratic. Try as they may, officials seem unable to predict the demand for trained people or to ward off strong political pressures in making their projections. Hence, there is little reason to prefer one system to another on grounds of accuracy. It does seem clear that a predominantly laissez-faire system like our own leaves young people more freedom to try to enter a profession. As a result, they are more willing to accept the consequences if their expectations are frustrated and less inclined to place the blame on the state. Whether these characteristics make our system superior to others is not an objective question but a matter of personal opinion. All that one can safely say is that our method conforms more closely to the values of our society than would a system dependent on central planning.

The public is also concerned with admissions policies. Professional schools serve as gatekeepers to the professions, and access to these callings has long been an important means of social mobility. Hence, groups aspiring to higher status have always pushed against the doors of the universities. On this score, faculties have performed reasonably well—at least recently. They have long made scholarships available to students of limited means. Since 1970, they have admitted women and minorities, and even encouraged them to enroll through aggressive recruiting, financial aid, and the use of admissions standards that consciously favor members of disadvantaged groups.

Beyond these contributions, professional schools face an array of further challenges arising from the callings they serve. None of the professions I have been considering stands in particularly high repute at present. Levels of public trust in lawyers, corporate officials, and physicians have declined markedly over the past twenty years, and confidence in the ethical standards of these groups has dropped substantially as well (although doctors have fared much better than lawyers and executives). To a large extent, these trends may reflect the general malaise that afflicted our country after Watergate and the Vietnam War. But it is also likely that the public has come to expect more from all powerful professions. These demands in turn have presented each calling with formidable problems.

America now has more lawyers relative to its population than any other major country in the world. And yet many people see our legal services as seriously maldistributed. Institutions and well-to-do individuals consider themselves to be burdened with too many laws and far too much litigation. Thus, companies feel caught in legal delays and red tape; schools, hospitals, unions, and even universities feel harassed by regulation; insurance companies and physicians react bitterly to mammoth jury awards. If institutions complain of too much law, however, the poor and the middle class often cannot find adequate legal services at tolerable prices. Indigent defendants are herded through the criminal courts to receive hastily negotiated prison sentences, while people of modest means find it hard to afford a lawyer even for simple legal problems.

The situation in medicine is somewhat similar. Fueled by new technology and funded by huge insurance programs, society's medical bills have grown steadily over the past quarter-century, rising from 5.5 percent to more than 11 percent of the gross national product. These increases, totaling hundreds of billions of dollars, have provoked a massive effort by government and private groups to find ways of slowing the rise in costs. Unlike legal services, adequate medical care is available to the vast majority of the population through a combination of public and private programs. Nevertheless, more than 25 million people still fall outside any of these schemes and often receive medical services only as charity cases. The quality of their care is generally substandard, and even their ability to get proper service in time of acute illness is in jeopardy due to the struggle to reduce costs. Once again, therefore, massive and expensive services coexist with the specter of privation for the poor and disadvantaged.

Business confronts problems quite unlike those of law and medicine. Envy and mistrust always surround those who devote their talents to making profits. For years, however, American executives enjoyed great respect for their efficiency and initiative. Today that confidence is imperiled by the well-publicized problems of competing with Japan and other industrialized and industrializing countries. At the same time, the public continues to have high expectations of large corporations in all aspects of their performance. People hold executives to higher ethical standards than they did generations ago, in the face of moral dilemmas that seem increasingly subtle and difficult as the economy grows more complicated. Politicians and opinion leaders call on companies to help address an array of social needs, from chronic unemployment to the financial problems of the performing arts. As the public has come to recognize the limits both of competition and of government regulation, different interest groups have increasingly pressed executives to move beyond the traditional preoccupations of management and respond voluntarily to the claims of minorities and women, the needs of the environment, the problems of the schools and inner cities, and many other issues.

By and large, professional schools have done very little to prepare their students to face these problems. They have given a low priority to teaching students to reason about the ethical dilemmas of practice or to consider the social problems facing their profession. Recently, more faculties have begun to offer courses on these subjects. Just as in the case of teaching skills, however, such offerings are usually optional courses taken by a small minority of students. Law schools are the sole exception, and even there, teaching professional responsibility has become mandatory only because a determined bar insisted on it.

Granted, taking a course will not transform future practitioners into ethical human beings or make them concerned and constructive members of their profession. But classes and readings can presumably help students understand the history of their profession, acquaint them with its principal needs and shortcomings, and expose them to the best available thought on appropriate steps toward reform. Courses in ethics can help students learn to recognize moral dilemmas when they arise, expose them to the best writings on the subject, and teach them to seek ethical means to accomplish their ends. Although there is no way at present of proving the point, it seems likely that such training will have a beneficial impact on the conduct of normally sensitive, conscientious students. Skeptics sometimes argue that courses do not build character and that teaching will not help those who have no concern for the interests of others or lack the willpower to put principle into practice. But similar criticisms can be leveled at all professional education. No amount of training will make an erratic person into a wise executive or turn a selfish individual into a caring physician. Education has never claimed to give students all of the qualities of character and judgment they need to perform well in practice. Yet this hardly means that professional schools should abandon their efforts to provide the best training they can. Everyone accepts this point in assessing professional education as a whole. It is a mark of the peculiar ambivalence toward ethics and social responsibility that sensible people still question their place in the curriculum on such flimsy grounds.

The low priority professional schools have tended to give these subjects seems especially unfortunate today. The social problems facing law, business, and medicine may be too large and complicated for the professions to cope with by themselves. But it is clear that the country will never overcome such problems without the active, enlightened cooperation of practitioners. Would anyone suppose that we can control health costs, while preserving high standards of care, without the help of physicians? The answer seems obvious. And yet, medical schools have rarely made a determined effort to educate their students about these problems, preferring to leave the task to the American Medical Association. Schools of law and business are guilty of similar neglect. As a result, faculties in all three fields have forfeited the role they might have played as a conscience for their professions.

The Satisfactions of Practice

The failure to address issues of professional responsibility has another worrying consequence of a much more personal nature. By placing so little emphasis on the history and problems of the profession or the obligations of the practitioner, faculties have overlooked an opportunity to help their students think more deeply about the vexing question of how they can find meaning in their work and career. This subject has assumed increasing significance over the years. To quote from a recent study of the American character:

> In the mid-nineteenth century small town, it was obvious that the work of each contributed to the good of all, that work is a moral relationship between people, not just a source of material or psychic rewards. But with the coming of large-scale industrial society, it became more difficult to see work as a contribution to the whole and easier to view it as a segmental, self-interested activity.[12]

Clearly, the meaning of work and career is an intensely private matter, and students and practitioners have to think through their own individual answers. Some may find themselves completely absorbed by the challenge of trying to achieve personal recognition and material rewards. Others may find a fulfilling enjoyment in the craftsmanship required for first-rate professional work. For most people, however, lasting satisfaction will require something more—some abiding sense of serving others in significant ways.

Universities cannot provide these answers for their students. What they *can* do is confirm the legitimacy and importance of

12. Robert N. Bellah, Richard Madsen, William M. Sullivan, Ann Swidler, and Steven M. Tipton, *Habits of the Heart: Individualism and Commitment in American Life* (Berkeley: University of California Press, 1985), p. 66.

the subject and to give students the readings and occasions that will allow them to think about it seriously. Much useful material is already available in the classrooms and libraries of professional schools. Lectures on the history of the profession give some notion of the origins of one's calling and its development through time. Courses on ethics and professional responsibility suggest ways by which the practitioner can be of help to others. Biography can bring to light exemplary lives that illustrate what it means, in the words of Oliver Wendell Holmes, "to live greatly" in one's profession. Already, individual professors may touch on these topics, deliberately or unconsciously, in the course of their teaching. What is lacking is a willingness on the part of the faculty as a whole to acknowledge such subjects as a proper part of professional education and to accept a collective responsibility for developing ways to help students think more productively about these important questions.

One can sympathize with the reticence of many faculties to assume this obligation openly. The meaning of one's work is an awkwardly personal subject. Many students may not be ready to consider it seriously. Many faculty members may inwardly wonder whether they have found enough meaning in their own lives to qualify them to discuss such issues with their students. Nevertheless, a faculty that does not make this subject a legitimate part of professional education ignores what for many students is undoubtedly the most important problem they will encounter in their professional lives.

In the end, any appraisal of our professional schools will depend very much on the yardstick we elect to use. Compared with their counterparts abroad, American schools look strong indeed. Their classes are interesting, their teaching innovative, their curriculum attuned to many demands of practice. Measured against the needs of their profession, however, performance falls noticeably short of the ideal, even after due allowance is made for the effects of cost constraints and intellectual barriers.

This assessment corresponds quite closely to what one would expect from studying the environment in which these schools operate. The fact that professional faculties in America are more exposed to pressure from their constituencies and freer to experiment with new programs and new forms of instruction has helped them to perform better than most of their counterparts abroad. At the same time, since competitive pressures are much weaker in matters of education than in research, our faculties have not felt great urgency in fully satisfying the legitimate needs of students, practitioners, and the general public. To this extent, they have failed thus far to accomplish all that they might.

In recent years, society's needs have increased, pressures for improvement have intensified, and faculties have begun to respond. Professors today are undoubtedly devoting more effort to teaching important skills and exposing more of their students to issues of ethics and social responsibility. These ventures are promising. By and large, however, they still exist at the periphery, outside the basic core of instruction. There is a cynical interpretation of their current status that tends to cast doubt upon their future prospects. In faculties of business, law, and medicine, the center of gravity has moved significantly over the past quarter-century from the practical interests of the profession toward the more abstract research orientation of the academy. Against this backdrop, clinical legal education and other ventures into skills training may be seen as efforts tolerated by the majority of professors in order to protect their continued preoccupation with more theoretical pursuits. Motivated in this way, faculties have not discouraged the new initiatives, but neither have they succeeded often in integrating successful experiments into the basic curriculum where most students will take advantage of them. So long as this situation prevails, the outlook for these subjects will remain precarious and important needs will still be only partially met.

4

New Developments

Soon after taking office in 1971, I chanced to dip into a stack of writings on the optimum size of a university. Some of the articles seemed tedious, but others were quite arresting. In one study, the president of a college set out to discover how large his student body could be and still permit a typical undergraduate to walk across the main quadrangle after an 11:00 A.M. class with a better than even chance of meeting at least two personal acquaintances. The researchers attacked this question with an awesome barrage of statistical techniques and left me only slightly more skeptical than I was when I began by concluding that the proper size for the college was exactly the number of students already enrolled.

The other studies I read did not start with such an inspired charge. But all of them sought to determine how much room a university has to maneuver between the Scylla of unrealized economies of scale and the Charybdis of excessive size. The usual answer was that the university needed at least five or six thousand students to provide a sufficient base for an adequate array of top-quality departments. Above fifteen thousand students, however, no further economies of scale seemed achievable. Institutions that exceeded this limit would have little to show for it save bureaucracy, inefficiency, and a growing loss of personal attention. Or so the experts said.

After studying these reports, I needed but a few moments to

discover that my own university already numbered fifteen thousand students. The total appeared to have crept up by some four thousand students in the previous decade alone, even though Harvard had not created any large new programs or professional schools during that period. Immediate action seemed to be called for. I swiftly issued memoranda to the deans urging them to hold their entering classes at existing levels unless they received my explicit permission to expand. We soon began counting students almost as carefully as we counted money and succeeded over the next ten years in clinging tenaciously to the total of fifteen thousand.

Flushed with this success, I was astonished one day to learn, almost by accident, that my enrollment freeze was more apparent than real. In addition to the fifteen thousand students "regularly" enrolled, forty-five thousand other people were coming each year to Harvard for some kind of formal instruction, many more than had come only a decade before. I was aware of our summer school, our extension courses, our midcareer executive programs. But I had never put them all together, let alone imagined that they could reach a total close to forty-five thousand students.

Who *were* these people, I wondered. The answers were intriguing. "These people" turned out to be unusually varied: salespersons and lawyers, housewives and business executives, shopkeepers and mayors. They came on weekends, in the evenings, in the summer—for a few days, a few weeks, a few months. Gradually, they were beginning to change the very nature of the institution. Without fanfare or debate, they were taking us back to the medieval university where people of all ages gathered to study.

This brief account suggests that important changes do take place in universities, sometimes without the knowledge or approval of campus officialdom. Some of these shifts result from emerging needs in the society, others from new ideas about education or new ways of looking at the world, still others from technological innovations. In the past fifteen years, three important changes have come about from just such causes: the growth of lifelong professional education, the emergence of new schools of public policy and administration, and the invasion of our campuses by computers.

Education for Professional Development

Nontraditional students of the kind that are flocking to Harvard come for many reasons: to get a foretaste of college, to test their interest in a particular vocation, to explore some subject for cultural reasons, to prepare for retirement. But the largest new growth in nontraditional study has occurred not for motives of this kind but for reasons connected with vocation and career.

In a few fields—at least at Harvard—groups of seasoned professionals come to the university for a full year to pursue programs pretty much of their own choosing. Journalists and diplomats are prominent in this category. Conceivably, their presence owes much to accident, the happenstance of a particular donor or the special interest of an enterprising professor. But there is probably more to the matter than chance. Both of these professions are demanding, having their fair share of minor crises and taxing work. At the same time, professionals in both fields can profit from stepping back to learn about subjects related to their work. Political reporters can write with greater depth if they have a better grasp of American history or an understanding of political theory; diplomats may have reason to know more about arms control, Far Eastern civilization, international economics, or any of a score of other subjects. For such people, a year of detachment and study can offer rewards that will last for a long time.

How many other callings exist in which practitioners can benefit in these ways? Some, undoubtedly. But the list is limited. A professional in any field may profit from taking a sabbatical from a busy practice to pursue private interests and to take stock. Yet few will find that a year of general study contributes as much to their working lives as it does for journalists and diplomats. Social workers, perhaps. Clergy and teachers, surely. But the number of candidates soon begins to dwindle. Most doctors do not need a year studying modern biology or the history of medicine, nor are many lawyers likely to feel that they have done much to enhance their careers by a semester spent reading philosophy, economics, or even constitutional theory.

Another group of midcareer students consists of people who have done outstanding work of a specialized kind in a large organization and are now awaiting promotion to broader, executive-level positions. This type of advancement occurs most frequently in corporations, in the military, and in the federal civil service. At such a critical juncture in their careers, these executives can profit from an opportunity to meet with professors and fellow students to discuss the kinds of problems they will face when they assume their new responsibilities. The point of the experience is not to learn a body of information, nor even to master specific skills, but to acquire a capacity to approach bigger, less specialized problems with a broader perspective and an openness to many different approaches and points of view. This type of transformation emerges most readily from an immersion of several weeks or months in the company of others who come from a wide variety of backgrounds—from different organizations, different industries, even different countries.

There are other professions in which established practitioners rarely shift to new and broader responsibilities; for the most part, they specialize throughout their careers. Lawyers in large firms typically follow this path, as do most physicians. Such people look to the university chiefly for programs of short duration that will help them keep up with recent discoveries or learn the latest skills. The growth of new knowledge has been accelerating rapidly in fields like law and medicine and has now reached floodlike proportions. Fortunately, technology is fast providing new methods of helping professionals search these mounds of data to find the information they need for specific problems. Television and computers allow doctors and engineers to learn new techniques and catch up on new developments without even having to leave their home or workplace. Still, practitioners must have more than a machine to put new developments in a broader perspective, to analyze emerging patterns, to synthesize information and extract a greater meaning. They often seek a forum in which to talk with colleagues under the guidance of knowledgeable instructors. These needs have accounted for the steady growth of short "refresher" programs in law and medicine ranging in length from a single weekend to a fortnight.

The oldest vocational reason for returning to the university is to acquire new skills or new knowledge to perform a different type of job. For generations, adults have flocked to extension courses to learn a language for assignment overseas, to master accounting for a business career, to study educational psychology for help in getting certified as a schoolteacher. In the last few years, the rising importance of the computer has attracted hordes of students wanting to become programmers.

For generations, students who came to learn a new skill studied at their own initiative for jobs they hoped to find at some future date. More recently, universities are beginning to attract groups of people who have already acquired a new and difficult job and feel the need for some organized preparation. This phenomenon is particularly noticeable in public life. People are often elected or appointed midway in their careers to positions of high responsibility for which they have little preparation. Congressmen, judges, mayors, and political appointees of various kinds all share this predicament. In earlier times, the adjustment to these jobs, though difficult, did not seem especially daunting. Within the past generation, however, many important posts have come to entail such complicated issues, such a volume of information, such sophisticated methods of analysis that many new officials feel the need for some form of systematic preparation.

The programs created to meet this demand are normally far too brief to accomplish much of substance. For newly elected public officials, in particular, the few days that participants can spare allow little more than a chance to remove some of the mystery surrounding their new jobs and to convey a few basic ideas about how to address their responsibilities. Still, it is noteworthy that they come at all. A generation ago, scarcely any elected officials would have thought it worthwhile to spend even a few days at a university for such a purpose. Today, more than two-thirds of all newly elected congressmen volunteer every other year to attend an intensive program at Harvard. In this, surely, there is promise of substantial opportunities to come.

Programs such as the course for new congressmen dramatize the change that has occurred in the reasons that inspire universities to offer nontraditional education. In the early days, most educators conceived such offerings as a form of community service—a way of giving instruction at little cost to those who could not afford to come to college or who felt a need to continue studying for cultural or vocational reasons. A second rationale, which spurred the growth of summer schools and later spread to other forms of nontraditional education as well, was the desire to use the university's physical plant more efficiently and thus spread fixed expenses. This motive grew especially powerful in the 1970s, when universities had to find ways of coping with inflation and government cutbacks after a quarter-century of prosperity.

The newer programs offer a reason for nontraditional education quite distinct from wanting to serve the community or improve the bottom line. So long as these older motives alone prevailed, most members of the university community merely tolerated continuing education courses provided they were taught by someone else and at times and places that did not interfere with the regular academic schedule. But now that political leaders, admirals, journalists, and other imposing figures are searching for university instruction, old attitudes are beginning to change. Few professors may show much interest in teaching accounting or computer programming in the evening. But who is to say that courses for newly elected legislators or freshly appointed judges are not as stimulating and important as lecturing to regular classes of students in college or professional school?

In the face of this new interest, we need to think more seriously about the proper place of continuing education in the university. And high time! When a university begins to attract nontraditional students in numbers several times the regular enrollment, it cannot go on squeezing in midcareer programs during weekends and vacations. The moment has come to reconsider the place of nontraditional programs in the regular work of the institution.

In order to treat this question seriously, we must stop thinking of people aged eighteen to twenty-five as the only "real" students. Instead, we need to compare the virtues and drawbacks of teaching younger and older persons without preconception or prejudice. To paraphrase George Bernard Shaw, why should all the benefits of youth be squandered on the young?

In fact, teaching younger students does have many advantages. The essential point is not that they are necessarily brighter and quicker (though they may have an edge in certain subjects, such as computers and calculus, that require a pure, abstract intelligence). A better argument is that education serves purposes for students at the beginning of their adult lives and careers that simply cannot be duplicated in later periods. A year's sabbatical may offer many busy adults an ideal opportunity for reflection and renewal. But four full years of college will rarely mean the same in middle age as they will earlier in life when students have so much to discover about themselves, their relations to others, their commitments to work and career. As a practical matter, moreover, college is almost always more appropriate for the young, since few individuals in midcareer can stop what they are doing and take four years to study the liberal arts.

In the case of professional education, the early training one receives is also uniquely important. Valuable as it is later on to learn of new developments in one's field or to broaden one's perspective, it is even more important to begin one's professional career by mastering the skills and knowledge that are essential to practicing at all. One can imagine an established lawyer, physician, or architect continuing to function without the benefit of further instruction. But it is difficult to conceive of ever trying a case, operating on a patient, or designing an apartment house without having had any formal professional training.

To say that the established forms of education for younger students deserve the priority they have received is not to imply that *all* such programs are justified. Nor does it mean that all these offerings must last as long as they do at present or that their enrollments must be as large. By looking carefully, we may discover that some traditional programs are too big or too long, demanding time and resources that universities could better use for the benefit of older audiences. This is a possibility worth exploring, for older students have advantages over their younger counterparts that are too important to go unrecognized.

Seasoned professionals who return to study in midcareer are often more highly motivated than younger students. Few of them would take the time and trouble to leave their jobs, even for a few weeks, unless they had a specific purpose they hoped to achieve at the university. They are not tired of papers and lectures, since few of them have attended a university for many years. For such individuals, the chance to study is a fresh experience, and they approach their programs with great interest and enthusiasm.

In contrast, traditional students have been going to school for so long that they are often jaded—weary of sitting through lectures and coping with assignments and exams. Some of them are not even sure why they are in the university. For example, a survey administered to entering law students at Harvard in 1970 revealed that more than 20 percent were certain they would never practice law while almost a quarter professed to be wholly undecided. While such students may still gain something from a university experience, many of them accomplish far less than they should and might do better to leave the familiar academic environment, at least temporarily, for a different kind of challenge.

Even when entering students are committed to a career in the profession, it is not at all certain how much of a contribution they will ultimately make. Conventional methods of selection, with their emphasis on prior grades and standardized-test scores, are only moderately useful in predicting a student's record in professional school, and none of these criteria have much value in identifying people who will do something important in their later careers. The contrast with midcareer students is striking. Established practitioners have firmly committed themselves to their calling. One can make fairly accurate predictions concerning their achievements in later life by examining what they have already accomplished. As a result, in choosing established practitioners the university stands a better chance of selecting students who will go forth and make significant contributions to their profession.

Older students have the added advantage of bringing with them a level of experience that is valuable to their teachers, particularly in professional schools. Most midcareer programs are taught by the discussion method, in which feedback from participants is immediate and full. In addition, there are usually ample opportunities for students to mix informally with their instructors. In these circumstances, the chance to teach experienced lawyers, architects, school superintendents, or business executives does much to keep a faculty in touch with the practicing profession and to prod instructors whose materials and methods have become too abstract or too dated to serve the needs of their audience.

The advantages of educating established professionals are significant enough to warrant greater efforts in this direction. How might we rearrange the existing offerings of the university to distribute educational opportunities over the entire life cycle in a manner most beneficial to students? Since universities cannot grow indefinitely, it is not enough simply to list new programs. We must also ask where to cut back traditional offerings to make room for more older students.

The undergraduate experience should continue to be the preserve of the young, for reasons I have already given. Suppose, however, that a university with several thousand undergraduates found it possible to attract a few hundred older students who were talented, well established in interesting careers, and eager to come for a year: journalists, diplomats, and clergymen looking for a period of study and reflection; lawyers, business executives, civil servants, and the like simply taking a sabbatical to pursue private intellectual interests. Suppose as well that the university did not wish to expand its student body any further.

If such a choice had to be made, a sensible faculty might well prefer the older students. Anyone who has talked to such people at the end of a year of study knows how much they value the opportunity. They also bring as much to the university as they take away. Much of the value of the undergraduate experience comes from the chance to know other people of widely varying backgrounds and talents. That is why most colleges put so much emphasis on attracting students from different races, geographical areas, occupational backgrounds, and income groups. Try as they may, however, colleges still constitute a sort of youth ghetto; their students are varied and interesting but almost all under the age of twenty-two. From this perspective, the opportunity to attract several hundred older persons from many different walks of life could hold great advantages. In discussions about coursework, current events, personal dilemmas, or career plans, the presence of accomplished, experienced adults would add a unique resource for a community in which even faculty members may have led quite specialized, circumscribed lives.

In professional schools, the opportunities to make room for older students are different and more numerous. Law schools provide a promising place to begin, since a number of prominent legal educators and bar groups have already urged that the basic preprofessional training is too long and should be cut from three years to two. Deans have resisted this notion, in part because they fear that the resulting drop in enrollments will drain resources from their schools. But a variety of useful programs for older lawyers could be designed to fill the gap. Some faculties could offer master's programs in complex fields of specialization—such as taxation, antitrust, or international law—especially in schools located in urban areas, which can attract local practitioners on a part-time basis. Eventually, a few law schools might even succeed in persuading the bench to encourage newly appointed judges to spend a few weeks or months of preparation taking advanced courses in evidence, procedure, and other relevant subjects. Still other faculties could offer programs to train paralegal personnel or to prepare mediators, arbitrators, and others to meet the growing demand for alternative ways of settling disputes.

These suggestions may seem radical. But experienced law teachers know how many third-year students are bored with their courses and how much their classes merely duplicate work already done to develop analytic skills. Since third-year students seem to perform no better than their second-year colleagues in the same courses, the final year does not appear to add much to students' reasoning abilities. Hence, unless law professors can invent something more valuable for the final year, they might make more of a contribution by using their talents to give further education to established practitioners with important functions to perform in their profession.

Schools of architecture present a different kind of opportunity. There is little doubt that universities are now graduating more architects than the profession can absorb. The faculties of existing schools are mainly staffed by distinguished practitioners who do little research and teach a curriculum inspired by the vision of training master designers in the tradition of Frank Lloyd Wright, Le Corbusier, and I. M. Pei. Alas, only a handful of students, even in the best schools, will ever get the chance to design beautiful buildings. Many will work for large commercial firms building ordinary structures under extremely tight constraints. Many will end up in government agencies evaluating other people's designs. And many will not find jobs in architecture at all.

The traditional pattern of educating architects is not immutably fixed. It is possible to conceive of a design faculty more concerned with research and capable of developing advanced work for practitioners beyond the first degree. Such a faculty could cut back the number of preprofessional students and begin offering concentrated midcareer courses for architects hoping to move to new kinds of specialized assignments, whether they be office buildings, hotels, or university facilities. More extensive offerings could be imagined for architects wishing to engage in the planning and design of much larger projects encompassing many buildings. Shorter, specialized courses might be given on such topics as new materials for construction, sophisticated methods of energy conservation, or uses of the computer in the design process. In this way, faculties could help to bring the supply of architects more nearly in line with the demand while doing a better job of preparing experienced practitioners for more complicated tasks.

Similar possibilities exist in the field of public management. In recent years administrators of large organizations outside the business sector have faced increasing challenges. Budgets are larger, staffs are bigger, employee relations are more volatile, and community pressures are more intense. These conditions prevail not only for officials who run government agencies but also for museum directors, school principals, hospital administrators, foundation officers, city managers, and many others. As in the corporate world, these executives have to administer with the greatest possible efficiency to avoid wasting scarce resources. But the skills they need are not exactly the same as those of the corporate manager. The institutions they direct have different missions, with goals that are harder to measure, time horizons that are shorter, and political pressures that are more intense. Thus, business schools are not necessarily the proper places for these administrators to get the training they need; faculties of education, public administration, city planning, and public health may have much to offer such students as well.

Successful programs already exist for almost all important fields of administration within the nonprofit sector. The potential value of such courses is great indeed, considering the social importance of schools, hospitals, and museums, not to mention government agencies. Effective programs can attract established professionals who hold—or soon will hold—substantial positions in these institutions. Surely the chance to help such people perform better may justify some selective pruning of traditional programs—even if that should mean cutting back on enrollments of the younger students who have traditionally populated our professional schools.

As universities continue to place more emphasis on attracting older students, they will find themselves competing with other kinds of institutions, such as corporations and professional groups, that offer instruction to established professionals. Indeed, in all of higher education, it is here that competitive pressures are likely to work most effectively. Established practitioners are more sophisticated, more aware of their needs, and better equipped to select a suitable program than recent college graduates who have not yet spent time in practice. If even these professionals cannot choose, the organizations that send them will undoubtedly step in and survey available programs in order to pick the ones most suited to their purposes. One way or another, therefore, universities will face an unusually demanding market.

In this environment, academic officials will face harder choices than they have had to make heretofore. Until now, progress in the continuing education of professionals has not come at the cost of established programs or demanded much of established professors. Only rarely has a need arisen to burden the regular faculty by pressuring them to teach in the new courses or to share facilities and resources. If anything, continuing education has been tacked on to existing activities, bringing added income to professional schools to help meet normal expenses.

Further progress will gradually call for more significant tradeoffs. In some cases, decisions to expand continuing education will require cutting back on traditional enrollments. The quality of programs needed to attract established professionals is also likely to demand more participation by the regular faculty and greater access to facilities at convenient times of the day, week, and year. Above all, universities that wish to succeed in midcareer education will have to recognize it as an integral part of their teaching program entitled to the same resources and the same care in development and supervision as more traditional activities.

Thus far, continuing education has achieved this status only in a few faculties. In medicine, for example, many states require that all doctors take a stipulated amount of continuing education. As a result, courses for practicing physicians are regarded as important, and medical schools, as well as professional organizations, have responded with an impressive array of instructional vehicles. Self-assessment materials enable doctors to test themselves to determine the subjects in which they need further study. Instruction is available in the form of home readings, teleconferencing, computer-assisted instruction, and cable television as well as the more familiar short refresher courses. In some schools even more elaborate opportunities are available. For example, Harvard Medical School alumni can return to the school for tutorials or miniresidencies lasting days or weeks in which they can study with regular members of the clinical faculty. Surveys reveal that a large majority of the clinical professors at Harvard engage in this or some other form of instruction for practicing physicians.

The development of midcareer education in schools of management is no less impressive. In 1950 only four business schools offered executive programs. The number ballooned to sixty a decade later and to ninety by 1970. Today, more than 80 percent of Fortune 500 companies send executives to university-based courses. At a business school such as Harvard's, students in these programs have their own classrooms and living facilities, and faculty members are assigned to executive classes as a regular part of their teaching obligation. Courses are not restricted to evenings, weekends, and vacation periods but occur during the regular academic year. In business as in medicine, midcareer education has become an integral part of the school's mission.

The great challenge of continuing education will be to make it central to the activities of every professional school without stifling the innovative, flexible qualities that have enabled it to grow so successfully in the past. As we have seen, the value of such programs can be considerable. By working hard to educate established practitioners, universities can make a distinct contribution to the professions while helping faculty members to remain in closer touch with the world of practice. In many cases it is the quality and diversity of the students and their manifest desire to learn that do the most to persuade universities to move in this direction. As business schools have discovered, the experience and interest of seasoned practitioners and the chance to help them fill important professional roles are opportunities too attractive to pass by. For schools that move in this direction, the effort to excel in such an exacting, competitive enterprise may bring improvements in the quality of instruction that will spread beyond continuing education to benefit the entire curriculum.

Education for Public Service

Among the many nontraditional students coming back to Harvard in the 1980s were public officials of every kind and description. Mayors, congressmen, generals, admirals, subcabinet officers—all had programs tailored to their interests, and all appeared in impressive numbers. Why were they eager to come? And why had they come so rarely in the past? To find answers, we must go back twenty years or more—to the era of the Great Society, to the New Frontier, and even to the New Deal.

The decade of the 1960s produced dramatic changes in the feelings of Americans toward their government and what it could accomplish. At the beginning of the decade, countless people were stirred by the thought that a new young president would "get the country moving again" and that bold federal programs could overcome poverty, urban blight, racial discrimination, unemployment, the arms race, and other national afflictions. The Model Cities Program, the Alliance for Progress, the War on Poverty, the Great Society were fetching symbols of a wide belief in the curative powers of money and government intervention. Scarcely a dozen years later, these hopes had already begun to flag. Billions of dollars had been spent, but the same problems remained. Worse yet, the public had experienced a cruel and divisive war, the scandal of malfeasance in high places, and levels of inflation and unemployment unmatched since the Great Depression. By the early 1970s, public confidence in the competence and integrity of government officials had dropped precipitously, and skepticism and disillusion had replaced the optimism of the Kennedy years.

The mood shifts of the 1960s were signs of a public seeking to come to terms with a vast metamorphosis in the role of government—a process that had begun during the 1930s and continued through World War II and beyond. During that time, the role of government had grown enormously. The New Deal created vast new public responsibilities for the domestic economy, while World War II propelled the nation into a position of international leadership.

This transformation vastly complicated the work of public officials. It was much more difficult to decide how to eliminate poverty or how to combine low inflation with high employment than it was to deliver the mail, administer the customs service, or conduct foreign policy as a small, isolated power. It was also much harder for a cabinet official to coordinate hundreds of separate programs, much harder to motivate and supervise a department with tens of thousands of employees, much harder to concentrate simultaneously on dozens of different crises and demands than it had been to administer the simpler public agencies of earlier times.

Because of these trends, it was apparent by 1970 that public officials faced a peculiarly difficult challenge. The powers they wielded had a critical effect on the lives of the entire domestic population, not to mention populations abroad. The issues before them were extremely complicated. Many of the agencies they relied on to implement their decisions had grown huge to the point of being impossible to administer. If Americans were disappointed by their government's performance, part of the explanation surely lay in the fact that the duties of public officials were more important, their problems more difficult, and their organizations harder to manage than those of any other profession in the society.

By the time the War on Poverty and the Vietnam War had come to an end, the size and complexity of government had been growing steadily for more than thirty-five years. Yet universities had not begun to make a serious effort to prepare people for the responsibilities of public office. In 1970, programs for public service did not approach in quality the training customarily given to those entering the professions of law, business, and medicine. Lacking a supply of able young people adequately prepared for government careers, federal agencies continued to rely on specialists at the lower and middle professional echelons—lawyers in the Justice Department, engineers in the Department of Transportation, economists and manpower experts in the Labor Department, and so forth. For overall management and policymaking, the executive branch still looked to political appointees, chiefly business executives and lawyers, just as it had for many decades. Able as many of these people were, they frequently lacked the training or experience needed to address the issues that faced them or to cope with the peculiarities of the political arena. And in an environment where the average tenure of an assistant secretary in a cabinet agency lasted less than two years, their terms of service were often too short to let them learn on the job.

Why did we lack great schools for public service comparable to our better faculties of law, business, and medicine? Part of the explanation undoubtedly lies in the low status of public service in America. In 1907, President Lowell rejected a proposal to found a school of public administration and opted for a business school instead, arguing that Harvard should not "be holding [itself] out as training men for a career that does not exist."[1] If government careers had enjoyed greater importance and prestige, distinguished schools might have developed. But in a country that looked upon government with suspicion and even disdain, the civil service never seemed as attractive to talented students—or to those who taught them—as it did in most countries of Europe.

Only with the coming of the New Deal did the government begin to attract young people with a desire to get involved in addressing large social problems. Even then, the pay and prestige were low relative to the major private professions. And the big jobs, the policymaking jobs, seemed almost always to go to outsiders, chiefly professors, attorneys, and corporate executives. An able young person with a taste for public issues had little to look forward to in government service; a career in law or business promised not only greater material rewards but also the chance of entering public life later on in a post of real authority and importance.

Pay and prestige were not the only reasons for the failure to develop strong professional schools in this field. In England, Germany, and other European countries, the public service was highly respected and offered coveted careers. Yet even these nations, France apart, never produced important schools of government administration. Instead, they relied on a classical liberal education or on legal training to prepare their government officials.

The most likely explanation for the lack of such professional schools is an intellectual one. Faculties found it hard to conceive of a challenging curriculum for public service—a body of knowledge and technique that could be more useful than a mere collection of facts and information about how government agencies functioned. Part of the problem was the amorphous

1. Letter from President A. Lawrence Lowell, quoted in Melvin T. Copeland, *And Mark an Era: The Story of the Harvard Business School* (Boston: Little, Brown, 1958), p. 6.

nature of the "profession." What single set of skills or common core of knowledge would possibly fit the extraordinary smorgasbord of jobs served up under the great tent of government? Another difficulty stemmed from our tradition of perceiving the public official as someone whose only task was to carry out policies devised by legislators and politically appointed officials. This conception appealed to our notions of democracy and separation of powers, since it assumed that policies were set only by officials directly responsible to the people. By 1970, however, and probably long before that, it was clear that career government officials did not merely execute policy but played an important part in its formation. But so long as this point continued to go unrecognized in the universities, the field of public administration did not convey much excitement or even lend itself to a coherent curriculum. One could piece together a study of familiar functions, such as personnel, budgeting, planning, and the like, or one could create a mixture of human behavior, organizational theory, social psychology, and other emerging subfields. But neither approach offered much of the excitement that might attract a student to public life, and neither provided a set of analytic techniques or special skills that could set graduates apart from other people as did legal training or, even more, a medical education.

As the Great Society drew to a close, therefore, it appeared that the growth in the size and responsibilities of government had outrun the abilities of officials who had to cope with our most significant national problems. The implications were not lost on professors who had gained first-hand experience in Washington. They recognized that there was a glaring weakness in American professional education, namely the lack of adequate programs to train capable people for careers in government service. Something had to be done to offer a quality of preparation equal to the challenge and importance of public life.

As this deficiency became apparent, the prospects for making an assault on the problem were already improving. Public service careers had gradually become more attractive, despite the passing disaffection produced by Watergate and the Vietnam War. The power wielded by government agencies and their involvement in addressing large social problems appealed to many young people of high ideals and personal ambition. At the same time, rising pay scales and civil service reforms were slowly making the prospects in government careers less discouraging. In the 1960s the idea began to spread that there was always a progressive government coming into its own somewhere—in states or cities if not in Washington—and that an enterprising person with the right contacts could move from one interesting job to another, getting in on "the action" as it moved around the country. Careful observers also began to note the rise of a cadre of "in-and-outers," able individuals who moved into policymaking posts when a congenial administration was in power and then moved out into universities, consulting firms, foundations, and assorted think-tanks when the government changed hands. As these alternatives grew clearer, talented, ambitious people had less reason to fear that public service would mire them forever in some stultifying government job.

While careers in government were growing more appealing, new methods of policy analysis were also starting to emerge, first from early work in operations analysis during World War II and then from projects at the Rand Corporation and similar organizations. These new skills moved with McNamara's whiz kids to the Defense Department and eventually spread to other agencies in Washington. Bright young staff people began to address complex problems with the help of sophisticated techniques, such as linear programming, cost-benefit analysis, and simulation methods. As officials began to use the new analytic methods in more and more government settings, it became possible to imagine a body of skills applicable to a wide variety of public positions. Perhaps these skills might be rigorous and difficult enough to provide the core of a respectable professional education. Intrigued by this possibility, professors at several universities went to work to create programs of public policy that could prepare people for important roles in government service. Within a few years, more than a dozen new ventures sprang up at institutions such as Harvard, Minnesota, Berkeley, Texas, and Duke.

The outlook for these new initiatives was not favorable in all respects. By the early 1970s the era of prosperity was over for higher education. Research funding had stopped increasing, inflation was on the rise, endowments languished in a sluggish stock market. Talk of retrenchment, not the creation of bold new educational ventures, was in the air. Besides, it was far from clear that the enterprise could succeed even if the necessary funds were found. Would able students want to come? Could a talented faculty be assembled? Was it possible to combine a set of analytic skills with a concern for better government to produce a solid curriculum?

With these uncertain prospects, universities had to make delicate choices among several possible strategies. The safest approach was to create a program of applied social science staffed by economists, statisticians, and political scientists with strong policy interests. This strategy minimized the problem of assembling an able faculty by appealing to professors in established disciplines who happened to have a taste for problems of government. Another advantage of such a program was that it could be mounted at almost any level of expense, beginning as a research institute for policy studies and evolving as circumstances permitted toward a full-fledged school of public service. The risks of failure were further buffered by the ability to integrate faculty members back into their parent departments if the new venture failed to attract enough students or foundered for other reasons.

Like many safe strategies, however, the program in applied social science (or policy studies) also promised limited rewards. The key problem had to do with the qualifications of economists, political scientists, and statisticians to prepare students for professional careers in government. The normal role of social scientists is to analyze activities and institutions to determine how they function, not to recommend practical steps to resolve policy problems. As scholars, they are usually more interested in establishing how the Cold War started than in fashioning ways to alleviate its tensions; in causes of crime rather than the choice of policies to contain it; in the consequences of welfare policies rather than their reform. Social scientists are also trained to gather all the available data to reach conclusions supportable by the standards of a professional journal; they are often uncomfortable teaching students to settle for the best solution obtainable with limited time and information. They are inclined to assume away the messy human failings of government and to feel uneasy with the political constraints and compromises that get in the way of fully rational decisions.

Because of these characteristics, building a program of instruction around social scientists held significant risks. At worst, such a faculty might produce analysts more qualified to discuss the problems of government than to recommend practical solutions. At best, students would be trained primarily as policy analysts and advisers for staff positions and not as executives in positions of authority and leadership. Such a school could play a useful role, but its contribution to government would be limited, just as a business school's role would be limited if it prepared its students only for positions on planning staffs and not for jobs with important line responsibilities.

A second strategy was to combine a program in public policy with a program in business administration to create an all-purpose school of management. On the surface, this alternative seemed appealing, joining a precarious new venture with a strong and proven partner. But it too presented high risks. For one thing, administering a government agency is very different from managing a private corporation. The goals of public agencies are more complex and amorphous; the time horizons are often shortened by impending elections and other political imperatives; the presence of rival agencies and different branches of government creates a host of special problems; the media may play a far more important role than they do in business. In public service, both the task of forming policy and the process of public management call for special skills and distinctive forms of analysis.

In a comprehensive school of management, there was a danger that these differences might be underemphasized. Because the business curriculum was so much older and more developed, because corporations offered students much more lucrative, predictable careers than government did, because it was much easier to raise funds for business administration, the corporate side of the school threatened to dominate. The public policy program would then be restricted to a handful of faculty, and most students would gravitate to the business courses. Since course material on corporate management was so readily available, the curriculum for public managers could also lean too heavily on business school precepts and cases without paying due attention to the peculiar features that distinguish government service from the operation of a private company. In such an environment, a strong program for public service might never have a proper chance to develop.

The third strategy was to establish a full-fledged school of public policy and public management with the explicit aim of preparing students for positions of executive responsibility at all levels of government. Such a school would stand alone. It could prepare its students with the help of three main groups of courses.

The first group would stress methods of policy analysis by teaching students to analyze a policy problem, to identify the alternative courses of action, and to determine the advantages and disadvantages of each. Professors would teach current analytic techniques drawn from economics, political science, statistics, and related quantitative fields. The aim would not be to train students to be specialists in linear programming or systems analysis. Rather, they would learn only enough to use such methods in addressing ordinary problems of moderate complexity. They would also be taught to be discriminating "consumers" of the techniques, able to understand them and know their capabilities yet also aware of their limitations.

The second cluster of courses would seek to prepare students to implement policies and manage complex government organizations. In the tradition of public administration, these courses would convey an understanding of basic tools such as prevailing methods of budgeting, institutional organization, personnel administration, and program evaluation. But the study of implementation would go beyond these subjects to consider how to assess the capabilities of an agency, analyze the political environment in which it operated, and muster support for its policies. To integrate these varied skills, professors would have their students work with elaborate cases or problems that would lead them to evaluate government agencies, analyze their environment, and devise effective strategies to achieve their objectives.

The third and final group of courses promised to be the most difficult to realize. Its aim would be to impart an understanding of humane values and ethical principles that would inspirit the process of policymaking and administration. To supply this perspective, the faculty could turn to materials drawn from moral and political philosophy, history, and the best of our legal and constitutional traditions. However hard to achieve, the ultimate goal of these courses would be to instill the appreciation of human values needed to enable public servants to maintain—and to deserve—the trust and confidence of thoughtful citizens.

Building a school along these lines presented difficult problems of its own. It would certainly be expensive, since it would require facilities and a faculty of substantial size without the ability to lean on a business school for support. In the early years, at least, such a school would undoubtedly face a dearth of qualified professors, since much of the curriculum would be new and would not come with a ready-made cadre of instructors willing and able to teach the necessary courses. This problem would undoubtedly create several risks. Frustrated by unsuccessful searches, a school could easily be driven to make most of its appointments in the fields where qualified professors were easiest to find, such as policy analysis and especially economics. In this event, the school would gradually transform itself into a program of applied policy studies, training people only for advisory and planning roles. In the alternative, the school might hire faculty who seemed to fill the necessary slots yet actually had a different orientation—business school professors to teach management and social scientists to teach policy analysis. In this event, the faculty might fail to train its students adequately for any of the tasks they were supposed to perform.

A faculty could overcome these risks through perseverance and good judgment. The same was not true of other hazards that beset these schools. For example, problems arose, and still arise today, from the uncertain nature of careers in public service. Graduating students can readily find exciting jobs assisting important policymaking officials. For several years, perhaps the first decade of their careers, such opportunities abound. But the transition to positions of line responsibility and the prospects for advancement thereafter present a great unknown. It is possible that society will produce enough intriguing private-sector jobs—in think-tanks, foundations, universities, and the like—to offer talented people a reasonable prospect for absorbing if changeful careers in and out of government. For less venturesome spirits, the career civil service—at least at the federal level—may gradually become professionalized enough to offer rewarding opportunities for continued development and responsibility. But these developments have not yet fully materialized. Until they do, schools of public policy cannot count on enrolling enough able and motivated students or on attracting faculties sufficiently talented to contribute substantially to the challenges facing the public sector today.

Another obstacle that faced the new schools in 1970, and one that still confronts them, is the inscrutability of so many important questions of public policy. Like it or not, no one today, however intelligent and prepared, has convincing answers for how to reduce crime substantially, how to combine full employment and low inflation, how to raise by very much the scholastic achievement of the nation's children, how to curtail teenage pregnancy or cure chronic unemployment or solve many of the other problems we expect our government to address.

One problem in thinking about such issues is that conflicts of value often lie at the root of the controversy. How many students should we be willing to flunk to impose higher academic standards in the public schools? Should we lower the minimum wage in the hope of providing jobs for more teenagers? How much should we rely on abortions to reduce illegitimate births among adolescents? Reasoned analysis can clarify the consequences of alternative policies, perhaps even find new possibilities that will avoid the clash of values. But often the conflict will remain, impervious to any analytic techniques that faculties can teach to students.

A second difficulty is that many policy issues are more complicated than they appeared to be in the past. Few important problems today seem merely technical or economic, as many did in the heyday of the New Frontier. Today, most issues seem rooted in murky questions of motivation, incentives, values, culture. Improving the nation's health depends on persuading people to alter their personal habits as much as on discovering cures for diseases. Combating poverty and chronic unemployment is not simply a matter of transferring money from rich to poor nor even of creating jobs; it requires an understanding of the culture of deprivation with its baffling array of disincentives and inhibitions. Providing housing for the poor no longer seems like a simple question of appropriating money to build public housing; it is haunted by the discouraging and puzzling fact that the expensive projects of the 1960s turned quickly into uninhabitable ghettos. Improving educational quality in the public schools requires a greater understanding of how children learn and why so many lack the motivation to study rather than a simple calculation of the cost of raising teachers' salaries and supplying new equipment. Crime, productivity, arms negotiation, and many more of our serious problems have much the same characteristics.

Such questions of motivation and behavior are much harder

than the technical problems of devising a social security system or an unemployment insurance program—considerably harder even than the task of guiding the economy, or instituting national health insurance, or resolving most of the other great public issues as they were commonly perceived during the first decades after World War II. As a result, schools of public policy have had to live with the realization that their stock of analytic tools may not suffice to create viable programs that can cope with many of our most important social problems.

Finally, these schools have had to come to terms with the same basic dilemma that has long troubled faculties of business. Experts on management still disagree on the qualities that make an outstanding manager. If this question is hard to answer for a private corporation, it is bound to be even harder in the complex political environment of the public agency. So long as the ingredients of successful leadership elude our understanding, it will be difficult to know how best to prepare young people for positions of administrative responsibility.

The many issues facing the fledgling schools of public policy illustrate the point that innovation in universities is not merely a matter of vision or of persuading faculty members to spare the time from their research to think about the education of their students. It can entail large amounts of money, much uncertainty, and substantial risk. In the case of public policy schools, the obstacles were large enough to deter most institutions from making a significant effort. Only a few universities tried to establish independent faculties. Several others took one of the safer paths of launching programs of applied social science or creating comprehensive schools of management.

More than fifteen years have now elapsed since the beginning of the public policy movement. Even this period is too short to allow an adequate assessment; schools of business and law took many decades to develop, and the field of public policy has not been favored by a particularly supportive national environment. Still, it may be possible even at this early stage to glean a few clues to help determine how to launch an effective program.

Thus far, at least, those who opted for limited strategies have had to settle for limited returns. Programs of applied social science continue to exist, but show few signs of expanding their curriculum to go beyond the study of policy questions. In some cases, their scope has actually narrowed to reflect an increasing dominance by economists. As for the comprehensive schools of management, their fortunes have progressed about as one would have predicted. Business education has come to dominate the faculty, the curriculum, and the student body. Typically, work on the public side has been confined to a few faculty members and a dwindling number of students. Although interest in government may eventually revive, there are few signs of growth at present.

In the case of the independent schools of public policy, I can write with confidence only about the one with which I have been closely associated, Harvard's Kennedy School of Government. In that institution, at least, there are several positive accomplishments. Recent college graduates admitted to the student body compare favorably in ability with those attending Harvard's older, well-established schools of law, business, and medicine. In order to hedge against the uncertainty of government careers, however, the number of these students is restricted, and almost one-third are engaged in joint programs with other professional schools. Offsetting these limited enrollments are several hundred midcareer officials who come each year to a variety of programs—for state and local officials, for senior career civil servants, for national security officers, and several more. For the most part, these students occupy positions of substantial responsibility and have more than enough experience to challenge their professors. Their presence offers a test of the curriculum's practical relevance and helps solidify the commitment of the faculty to offer genuine professional training.

The curriculum has been built in large part on cases and problems drawn from actual experience. Since some important fields, such as management and ethics, are still in early stages of development, the materials are in constant flux. Nevertheless, the positive response of established professionals in the midcareer programs gives some assurance that the instruction has value for the kinds of problems officials face in their professional lives.

The search for experienced faculty has proved very difficult, as expected, especially in new fields such as public management. Fortunately, help has come from an unexpected quarter. Despite the risks to their careers, extremely talented young faculty members, drawn by their interest in important issues of public policy, have been willing to come as assistant professors. As these new recruits develop, the problems of finding senior faculty promise to ease a bit, though not entirely.

Finances too have proved to be less of a problem than was originally feared. For several years, potential donors, especially from the corporate sector, seemed to be seized by the ancient fear that better training for public servants would only produce more resourceful bureaucrats with larger interventionist ambitions. Over time, however, these attitudes have changed as more and more people seem to have realized that government is already so large and so important that everyone has more to lose from inept and poorly trained officials than from clever, overreaching bureaucrats.

It is harder to judge the effects of the gaps and imperfections in our knowledge of policy issues and public management. The problems involved are undoubtedly serious. The depth of the education one can give to students must suffer from the difficulty of knowing how to resolve conflicts of value, where to find an acceptable theory of human nature, how to build useful generalizations about effective management. But these are not problems unique to public administration; they confront all faculties in fields like business, law, or education that concern themselves with human organizations and policies. Although the handicap is serious, it is nevertheless possible to teach students a form of disciplined analysis and a body of useful techniques that will help them to think more systematically and effectively about most of the questions that will confront them in their ordinary work. Moreover, the very existence of these new schools serves to mobilize the energies of talented faculties to whittle away at our ignorance and improve our understanding of government and how its powers can be put to optimum use. The products of this work should eventually prove valuable to public servants while strengthening the curriculum for students. That at least must be our hope. Because of the immense importance of government, few academic endeavors seem more deserving of our faith and encouragement.

The Computer Revolution

In the past few years, all across the country, newspaper articles and headlines have signaled the onrush of a new technology that promises to bring about changes in the practice of education very different from those I have discussed heretofore. Educational institutions everywhere are announcing programs that emphasize the computer. Colleges, libraries, business schools, faculties of engineering and medicine have all moved in this direction, often with ambitious projects and hardware costing millions of dollars. Enthusiasts can hardly restrain themselves in predicting the impact of these machines. According to the president of Johns Hopkins, Steven Muller, "We are, whether fully conscious of it or not, already in an environment for higher education that represents the most drastic change since the founding of the University of Paris and Bologna . . . some eight or nine centuries ago."[2] Because of the speed and accuracy of the new machines in performing mathematical computations and processing information, Ray Neff, former director of computer services at Dartmouth, can predict that "what Ph.D.'s did 25 years ago will be term projects for Dartmouth students."[3] "I'm not convinced there will always be a book," says Frederick Kilgour in describing the electronic library of the future.[4] Adds

2. Steven Muller, "The Post-Gutenberg University," in *Colleges Enter the Information Society,* Current Issues in Higher Education, 1983–84, no. 1 (Washington, D.C.: American Association for Higher Education, 1983–84), p. 32.

3. Ray Neff, quoted in Charles Kenney, "Plugged In," *Boston Globe Magazine,* December 9, 1984, p. 33.

4. Frederick G. Kilgour, quoted in Judith Axler Turner, "Electronic Library Planned for Researchers," *Chronicle of Higher Education,* November 14, 1984, p. 16.

Patrick Suppes, one of the pioneers in computerized instruction, "One can predict that in a few more years millions of [students] will have access to what Philip of Macedon's son Alexander enjoyed as a royal prerogative: the personal services of a tutor as well-informed and responsive as Aristotle."[5] Amid this euphoria, it is sometimes hard to sort out just what influences the new technology is likely to have, in the near future, on the nature of education in the university. But useful applications do exist, and several of them seem especially promising.

Saving Time

Many uses of the computer are chiefly designed to save time or to eliminate disagreeable chores. Electronic bulletin boards spare students the burden of finding announcements in campus newspapers or dropping by departmental offices. On-line catalogs save a trip to the library reading room. Word processing avoids the trouble of typing new drafts, while remote-site TV can take away the need to travel from home to campus.

One cannot be sure whether applications like these will actually improve learning or merely offer the student less drudgery. It all depends on how students use the time technology saves them. In many cases, however, educational benefits will unquestionably occur. In business schools, for example, the power of the computer not only helps students to avoid tiresome routine; it allows them to grapple with more complicated, realistic problems, using linear programming and other sophisticated analytic techniques that were not previously feasible for homework assignments. In architecture, computer-generated models reduce the time and skill required to complete a drawing so that students can experiment with many more ways of solving design problems. In undergraduate writing courses, word processing does not merely avoid the drudgery of retyping papers; teachers are now much freer to ask students to revise and rewrite until they submit a polished piece of work. In all these

5. Patrick Suppes, "The Uses of Computers in Education," *Scientific American* 215 (September 1966): 207.

cases, time previously spent doing dull, repetitive tasks can now be devoted to thinking about much more challenging, important questions.

Computer-Assisted Instruction

The new technology often comes with software expressly designed to improve learning. One of the most common methods is called computer-assisted instruction (CAI). A simple example of such a program is the following:

COMPUTER: Who was the first president of the United States?
1. Thomas Jefferson.
2. George Washington.
3. Abraham Lincoln.

STUDENT: Abraham Lincoln.

COMPUTER: Sorry. Abraham Lincoln was President of the United States during the Civil War from 1861–65. The first President served from 1789 to 1797 and had previously been Commander-in-Chief of the Continental Army during the American Revolution. Would you like to try again?

STUDENT: George Washington.

COMPUTER: Good work.

Computer-assisted instruction, of course, can also take more sophisticated forms. For example, the program can ask a few initial questions and, depending on the quality of the answers, branch automatically to material of a difficulty appropriate to the student's level of ability and comprehension. Some programs respond to wrong answers by taking the student back through the problem step-by-step to discover the source of error. Others appear as games to motivate the student. For example, instructors in French courses have used a program modeled on poker whereby teams are "dealt" questions and get points for giving correct answers.

Such exercises have several advantages as a supplement to

regular classwork. Students have to think and cannot merely read passively to take in information. They can practice when they wish and for as long as they wish. They can proceed as rapidly or as slowly as they please, moving on to new material only when they have mastered what has gone before. Well-crafted programs give students all the help and added explanation they need and automatically move to levels of difficulty appropriate to the learner. By instantly recording whether each response is correct or not, the computer allows students to recognize areas in which they need to do further work while alerting the instructor to problems that the entire class has encountered in mastering the material. In all these ways, the machine can adapt to the special needs of each learner and offer feedback of a kind rarely available in conventional courses.

Despite these advantages, CAI has major limitations. The student must answer the precise question posed by the machine and choose among the limited number of responses that appear on the screen. There is no room in this format for challenging students to define the problem for themselves, to explore a new hypothesis of their own, or to speculate about the material under study. Because of this characteristic, CAI is chiefly used to help students learn facts, basic routines (as in mathematical computations), or collections of rules. For universities, the principal applications have been in areas such as learning the rules of grammar, the principles of accounting, the elements of anatomy, and other bodies of basic information. With imaginative software, CAI may well stimulate students to learn more actively and master basic material more thoroughly than they would if they were taught only by conventional methods.

Socratic Dialogue

Instructors would also like to use computers to help students develop higher levels of thinking. Ideally, a computer would be programmed to act like Socrates, rarely giving answers but constantly challenging students with new questions in an ongoing dialogue. Unfortunately, technology is not advanced enough at present to permit such conversations. For one thing, it is not possible to anticipate all the responses a student might give to a complex problem so as to prime the computer to respond with further questions. Experts are also unable to program computers to understand the countless variations of ordinary conversation or to comprehend analogies, metaphors, and other common turns of phrase. As a result, the computer can carry on a dialogue only by using multiple choice or some other device to limit the number of permissible answers. This procedure significantly restricts the discussion, for one of the most important benefits of a Socratic exchange is to force students to think of their own responses instead of simply choosing from a predetermined list. Even so, a computerized dialogue using multiple choice can still encourage a student to think more rigorously than is possible under a traditional CAI program, since the machine does not answer yes or no but simply gives another question that forces the student to ponder the problem more deeply. At the same time, because such programs are more complicated, they are also much harder to prepare. Thus, the challenge will be to find instructors clever and dedicated enough to work out imaginative responses to all of the answers that students might give in even this restricted form of mechanized dialogue.

Expert Systems

A different way of teaching higher-level reasoning comes from so-called expert systems. One of the best-known examples is MYCIN, a computer program that can rival specialists in diagnosing bacterial infections in the blood and prescribing appropriate treatments. The core of the program consists of a few hundred rules that take the form: "If X is true, then ask the following questions or take the following action." These rules were created after long interviews with acknowledged experts to discover how they would go about making diagnoses and prescribing treatments. Physicians can use such systems as a check on their own clinical judgments. Armed with the MYCIN program, the computer asks questions about a patient, and the doctor answers with the appropriate data. The computer continues to seek information until it is able to arrive at a conclusion, which the doctor can then compare with his own judgment.

Expert systems like MYCIN can be adapted for educational use. Students not only can observe how the "expert" goes about solving problems but can interrupt and ask the computer to explain the steps of its reasoning and why it reached a particular conclusion or asked a particular question. In this way, the computer permits students to have greater access to an experienced "mentor" and to question it in more detail than is normally possible in real life.

Like all programs, expert systems have disadvantages and limitations. They are expensive to produce. They do not force students to solve problems for themselves but merely ask them to supply data and observe how the computer responds. Above all, such systems work only for a limited range of problems in which the knowledge involved is sufficiently structured, the possible relationships are sufficiently finite, the inferences and conclusions are sufficiently probable that programmers can deduce a series of rules with which to search for information, make and check hypotheses, and eventually reach a conclusion.

Simulations

Some of these limitations can be overcome by another form of computer application, the simulation. In medical schools, for example, a program can be created to simulate a live patient. Students can then ask the computer questions and order tests to gain the information needed to diagnose the illness. With such a program, the role of the machine is entirely different from what it is in the other applications I have described. The computer does not pose questions or control the dialogue; it simply acts as a repository of information, a model of reality that students can explore and analyze in order to define a problem, develop and test hypotheses, and eventually arrive at a reasoned solution. If an expert system is added to the program, a student who gets stymied can ask for help at any point, and the computer will tell the student what information to seek and why that information is important in light of what is already known. Further commands will lead the computer to summon detailed information on any aspect of the problem to help the student make a diagnosis.

Simulations, using videodisc or simply computers, can serve many other purposes. They can teach law students to interview witnesses, help business students learn to diagnose a company's marketing problems and recommend solutions, or even offer graduate students a wealth of data to use in constructing a research design to test hypotheses about social behavior. The strength of these programs is the opportunity they give for students to think for themselves in defining the problem and in reasoning toward a solution.

Still other programs simulate environments that are either too dangerous, too expensive, or too remote and inaccessible for humans to encounter directly. For example, with the help of computer graphics, undergraduates can observe the path of the moon circling the earth and conjure up changes in the mass or velocity of the moon in order to observe the effects of gravity on the shape of its orbit. Chemistry students can conduct simulated experiments on their TV screens combining substances too dangerous for laboratory use. Biology majors can watch simulated fruit flies breed at an accelerated pace and try to deduce genetic rules from the results. Medical students can observe the workings of the circulatory system and see how the removal of blood or the cutting of the nerve that regulates blood pressure will affect the functioning of the entire system. All these cases allow students to visualize phenomena that would otherwise remain abstract and to manipulate variables and observe their effects in ways that help them gain a more thorough understanding of concepts and processes that would otherwise seem remote and hard to understand.

All of the applications just described are simply illustrations of what is currently feasible in a rapidly changing field. New discoveries could quickly create added possibilities. If an inexpensive optical scanning device became available, students and faculty could soon conjure up on their TV screens virtually any book in the university library, or indeed in any participating library. If improved authoring systems were devised, instructors could prepare better software with much less effort, and the quantity and quality of computerized material would probably rise substantially. If we could understand the art of dialogue better, teachers might be able to program the computer to conduct more challenging discussions with students. No one knows when or even whether these developments will occur. The one thing that does seem certain is that new applications will emerge tomorrow that no one can foresee today.

Obstacles and Opportunities

Despite these intriguing possibilities, we must remember that technology has raised great hopes on several occasions in the past only to disappoint its backers. Thomas Edison once predicted that the phonograph would revolutionize teaching, and several prominent foundations and corporations spent large sums in a futile effort to bring radio and later television into widespread classroom use. In each case, the new technology foundered because it cost too much, aroused the opposition of teachers, and failed to deliver the pedagogic gains that its enthusiasts had promised.

Could computers meet a similar fate? The costs are certainly substantial enough to inhibit widespread use. Although the price of machines has historically dropped by a staggering 25 percent each year, the heavy expense of producing software and maintaining the equipment promises to keep the total cost at a high level for the foreseeable future. Computers, so much more versatile than television sets or radios, might also make instructors fear for their jobs. Yet neither of these inhibitions seems great enough to stop the computer in its tracks. Many universities have already shown a willingness to spend large sums in putting technology to educational use, and computer companies are prepared to help subsidize the initial cost in major ways. As for displacing teachers, computers do not pose a serious threat since they clearly seem destined to supplement professors rather than make them obsolete.

The third obstacle to technology is a more intriguing one, for there are still skeptics who question whether machines enhance learning. According to Richard Clark, a leader in evaluating educational technology:

> Five decades of research suggest that there are no learning benefits to be gained from employing different media in instruction, regardless of their obviously attractive features or advertised superiority . . . The best current evidence is that media are mere vehicles that deliver instruction but do not influence student achievement any more than the truck that delivers our groceries causes changes in our nutrition.[6]

What Clark must mean is that technology rarely gives instruction of a kind and power that cannot be duplicated by more conventional means. Thus, the questions and answers contained in most computer-assisted instruction could also be provided, albeit in more awkward form, by a cleverly arranged workbook. The computer simulations that help develop diagnostic skills might be given by a live tutor who acted as a patient and responded to questions until students could make an accurate diagnosis. Expert systems, like MYCIN, could be duplicated by simply letting a student watch a real expert go about solving difficult problems. Much of what computer graphics provide could be approximated in only slightly more cumbersome ways by the clever use of mock-ups, videotapes, and film strips. In principle, therefore, the new technology seems unique only in allowing students to address certain kinds of problems with greater depth and sophistication through its speed and power in manipulating data.

If this were all that could be said for the new technology, one

6. Richard E. Clark, "Reconsidering Research on Learning from Media," *Review of Educational Research* 53 (1983): 450, 445.

would wonder whether universities and their corporate patrons had lost their minds by spending scores of millions of dollars on such equipment. But there are other points to consider before making a final reckoning. To begin with, although most advantages of technology *can* be duplicated by conventional methods, few of them *will* be achieved without the new machines. Instructors could spend two hundred hours preparing for a traditional class, just as they must often do to develop an hour of computer-assisted instruction. But rarely will they actually do so. Medical schools cannot supply individual tutors patient enough to give each student endless practice developing diagnostic skills. Nor will distinguished specialists be available on call to explain how they reason step-by-step to reach a diagnosis. With student-faculty ratios of twenty or thirty to one, a law school professor cannot work with individual students, as a computer can, to check their progress in understanding basic material. And laboratory time will seldom be available to permit science majors to repeat difficult experiments as often as they can by running them in simulated form on their computer.

In short, the opportunities that technology makes possible have great potential for overcoming some important deficiencies in traditional forms of teaching. At present, most instruction in our universities is extremely passive and relies too much on lectures. Such forms of learning have grave limitations. In the words of a recent report for the National Academy of Science, "Cognitive research confirms that knowledge and skills learned without conceptual understanding or functional application to problems are either forgotten or remain inert when needed in situations that differ from those in which they were acquired."[7] Accordingly, universities need to adapt their teaching methods to encourage habits of critical thinking, of perceiving issues

7. "Report of the Research Briefing Panel on Information Technology in Precollege Education," in Committee on Science, Engineering, and Public Policy, *Research Briefings 1984 for the Office of Science and Technology Policy, the National Science Foundation, and Selected Federal Departments and Agencies* (Washington, D.C.: National Academy Press, 1984), p. 21.

clearly, of drawing sound inferences and generalizations from bodies of data. Because the new technology can challenge the student with problems, allow repeated practice in finding solutions, and give immediate feedback, it is able to provide exactly the kind of educational experiences that can fill these needs.

Even if technology failed to improve the learning process, students would still benefit from a chance to learn how to work with computers—or at least understand their uses and limitations—in order to prepare for their careers. With the waves of technical information that are engulfing medical practice, physicians will have to use these machines to summon up the data they need and manipulate it to aid them in reaching clinical decisions. Corporate executives already call on sophisticated computer analyses in reaching many business decisions. Even lawyers use computers to do their research and may increasingly look to expert systems for help in making certain kinds of professional judgments. More and more, therefore, professional schools will need to introduce computers, if not to improve the quality of instruction, then to familiarize their students with the technology and make them reasonably proficient in its use.

Thus far the balance of benefits and risks seems to favor the new technology. There is yet another consideration that tilts the scales even more decisively in this same direction. As I pointed out in earlier chapters, universities do surprisingly little to understand the ways in which students learn. Faculties rarely come together to think collaboratively about the educational process, and when they do, they almost always discuss what students should read and study rather than how students learn and how they might be helped to learn more effectively. For a variety of reasons, investigators in and out of universities have shown much greater interest in experimenting with computers to improve the learning process. By their power and versatility, the new machines have enlivened the field of cognitive psychology and turned the energies of many scientists toward artificial intelligence and its applications to learning. Because of the commercial possibilities, corporations are willing to encourage this process by investing large sums in research and development and by giving attractive discounts to universities. Professors, in turn, are impressed by the power of the computer, and many have become proficient in its use through their research activities. Some of them, at least, are tempted to try using the new technology to improve their courses. As more and more students enter universities knowing how to use computers, they will expect their instructors to use technology in their teaching and will press them to do so and even show them how.

This growing interest in many quarters may well be the greatest educational benefit of the new technology. As more people begin to use technology in the classroom, they are bound to think more carefully about the best ways to help students absorb new knowledge and master new intellectual skills. One simply cannot produce good software for teaching without paying close attention to the details of how to present the material to enhance learning and sustain student interest. This is not characteristic of traditional instruction. For most professors, lecturing requires much knowledge and a fair amount of organization but little conscious thought about how students actually learn. The same is true of many seminars and tutorials. In contrast, the task of designing educational software cannot go forward in this manner; every step of the process must be taken with a careful eye to its effect on the student, or the program will not work effectively.

This critical difference probably accounts for most of the gains in speed and effectiveness of learning often attributed to computer-assisted instruction. It is not necessarily the machines that produce these gains. In fact, there are experiments that seem to show that the machines are *not* primarily responsible. More likely, the improvements in learning occur because of the increased time and thought that enter into preparing the programs. Either way, however, students stand to benefit.

These prospects are inviting. Yet success is not guaranteed and may never be achieved because of the effort required to develop good instructional applications and to learn enough to use them. For all the experiments and publicity, we still do not have enough first-rate software. Most of the programs available today are basic drill-and-practice routines that resemble expensive electronic workbooks rather than the more imaginative examples I have described. Small wonder, in view of the many hours required to prepare a program for even a single hour of instruction. To surmount this barrier, university administrators will have to do much more than shower their campuses with expensive equipment in the hope that innovations will spontaneously occur.

A vital step will be to persuade some of the most respected members of the faculty to take an active interest in the new technology and to give them the funds and technical help they need to develop imaginative applications. As in so many human enterprises, choosing the right participants will be crucial. By and large, the most dedicated teachers will have thought the most about how students learn, but the leading scholars are more likely to command the greatest respect among their colleagues. Fortunately, there are almost always a number of faculty members who are distinguished both as teachers and scholars and feel deeply committed to both endeavors. The challenge will be to find ways of persuading these professors to participate in the use of new technology and to give them suitable recognition for doing so.

A second step will be to search for economies of scale in the production of software. It is neither feasible nor wise to expect professors to spend two hundred hours developing each hour of instruction for a small group of students. Campus officials will need to move aggressively to market software to other institutions to expand the audience and increase the rewards for first-class programs. At the same time, supporting services will be needed to make sure that professors can confine their efforts to the most creative work and do not have to waste their time performing tasks that can be delegated to others.

Finally, deans and other academic leaders will need to take an active part in making sure that new experiments are carefully evaluated. Despite all the publicity, most assertions about how much computers can improve critical thinking or speed up learning rest on still unproven hypotheses. Each new program should receive a careful review to determine whether it does in fact help students learn more quickly, or reason better, or understand new material more thoroughly. There is also much more we need to know about the new technology. In what circumstances does it motivate students more than conventional instruction does? Does CAI help some students more than others? Do the use of graphics and the chance to visualize and manipulate abstract phenomena increase comprehension?

Faculties and educational leaders should all have ample reason to evaluate the new technology. Because of the cost of using computers, administrators will surely want some way of deciding whether they can justify the expense. Curiosity should lead some professors to investigate the results of their efforts to use computers. Skeptics may ask why instructors should be any more interested than they have been up to now in trying to measure the effects of their teaching. Yet the climate for conducting such evaluations seems much more promising than in the past. For one thing, the interactive nature of computers will make it much easier for professors to acquire immediate information about the success of many of their electronic experiments. For another, it is much less threatening to assess the effectiveness of computer-based instruction than it is to inquire into more traditional methods of teaching. The first merely involves evaluating the effects of a machine; the second calls in question the value of the faculty members themselves. The first may simply result in canceling an order for new microcomputers; the second carries the more ominous prospect of either causing professors to feel ineffective or forcing them to change their methods of teaching. With ingenuity, then, and a modest use of funds, a determined administration may succeed in making careful evaluations of the new technology that will help everyone to use it with discrimination.

All things considered, therefore, and putting aside the exaggerated claims and the media hype, we can still look positively upon the new technology. With enough effort, universities should be able to use this equipment to engage students in a more active process of thinking and problem-solving that will improve their learning. In addition, computers may be a catalyst to hasten the development of new insights into human cognition and new ways of helping students learn. In many ways, this last possibility is the most intriguing. It remains an anomaly that professors spend so much time evaluating and criticizing other institutions yet devote so little effort to finding ways to improve their own educational programs. If technology can help in encouraging such an effort, that is reason enough to welcome its appearance.

The new developments described in this chapter are by no means minor changes. They address issues of basic importance: what kinds of students should be enrolled and at what ages? what do they most need to learn? by what methods will they be taught? The fact that matters of such importance are being discussed and that much change is already occurring are signs of genuine vitality in our universities. Nevertheless, most of the initiatives I have discussed remain at an early stage—still precarious, still operating at the margins of the institution, still lacking an accepted place in the established programs of the university. In this respect, the current state of midcareer education, public policy programs, and the use of computers has something in common with the situation we discovered in the major professional schools. Much ferment and experimentation have emerged from changes arising in the outside world. Yet it is still not clear that these initiatives will succeed in moving from the periphery to the center of the institution, gaining the status and resources that will allow them to make their full contribution and enjoy a secure and lasting life.

5

Prospects for Change

Mindful of the need to think creatively early in my administration, I quickly set about accumulating a list of what I thought were splendid ideas, great and small, to improve education at Harvard. I concluded that the time had come to clarify the goals of undergraduate education and to fashion a curriculum appropriate to those ends. I resolved that the new program in public policy should become a major professional school with its own buildings and independent faculty. I decided that the teaching of ethics deserved a more prominent place in the undergraduate curriculum, and in the professional schools as well. I conceived of several useful projects that Harvard should carry out: a center to help graduate students and junior faculty improve their teaching; a catalog packed with information culled from student evaluations that could inform instructors and assist undergraduates in choosing their courses; a study of the changes wrought by four years of college on the minds and attitudes of students . . . and other notions now faintly remembered.

At the end of two years, none of these ideas had taken root. True, no one had rejected them explicitly. But no one had embraced them either, and I lacked the time or, in many cases, the authority to implement them effectively by myself.

At this point, I felt disheartened. I could accept disagreement, even outright rejection, but silence followed by inaction seemed peculiarly frustrating. In true academic fashion, I sought guidance from the writings of those more versed in administration than I. By chance, a book on the college presidency had just appeared. I quickly devoured it. Stripped of its supporting charts and survey data, the authors' message was starkly conveyed in the following sentence: "The college president is an executive who does not know exactly what he should be doing and does not have much confidence that he can do anything important anyway."[1]

Clearly, this was a passage I should have read *before* accepting my current post; it was of little use to me now. I turned instead to the writings of a distinguished educator, Clark Kerr, who had earlier produced an excellent book on the modern university. Kerr too discussed the role of the president and closed his analysis with this trenchant summary:

> He wins few clear-cut victories, he must aim more at avoiding the worst than at seizing the best. He must find satisfaction in being *equally* distasteful to each of his constituencies; he must reconcile himself to the harsh reality that successes are shrouded in silence while failures are spotlighted in notoriety. The President of the multiversity must be content to hold its constituent elements loosely together and to move the whole enterprise another foot ahead in what often seems an unequal race with history.[2]

I laid Kerr's book aside. Enough of the realist school of academic administration.

In desperation, I reached for F. M. Cornford's classic essay offering advice to younger academic colleagues. Although I knew that Cornford would not tell me how to implement my ideas, I could surely depend on him to explain away my difficulties with characteristic wit by blaming them all on the conservatism of the faculty. Opening the book, I found much solace in his wry observations, until at last I came upon the following passage: "You think (do you not?) that you have only to state a reason-

1. Michael D. Cohen and James G. March, *Leadership and Ambiguity: The American College President* (New York: McGraw-Hill, 1974), p. 151.

2. Clark Kerr, *The Uses of the University* (Cambridge, Mass.: Harvard University Press, 1963), pp. 40–41.

able case, and people must listen to reason and act upon it at once. It is just this conviction that makes you so unpleasant."[3] This observation struck uncomfortably close to home. I decided to read no more.

Several years later, reflecting on the state of the University, I suddenly realized that almost all my early suggestions had now more or less come into being. Fortunately, I had been able to appoint as Dean of Arts and Sciences the faculty colleague who had first made me think about the inadequacies of the College curriculum. A basic reexamination of undergraduate education was soon under way. For one or two of my other ideas, money and perseverance had done the trick. More often than not, however, my proposals had simply vanished, gone underground, only to reappear unexpectedly a few years later with new advocates and new impetus.

Pondering this result, I wondered: Whose ideas *were* these now that they had undergone this process of hibernation and reawakening? Perhaps it was wiser not to ask. As Kerr once remarked, "innovations sometimes succeed best when they have no obvious author."[4] And yet, although the credit for new ideas scarcely matters, there is value all the same in trying to understand how progress actually occurs. Otherwise, we can have no hope of acting deliberately to bring about needed reforms.

The subject of change in universities produces radically different reactions from different observers. According to Irving Kristol (writing in 1968), "The university has been—with the possible exception of the post office—the least inventive (or even adaptive) of our social institutions since the end of World War II."[5] Yet only a few weeks before Kristol wrote, Jacques Barzun proclaimed with equal severity that "since 1945 the universities have been doing nothing but innovate—take on [projects] they had no ability or means of performing, and that's

3. F. M. Cornford, *Microcosmographia Academica: Being a Guide for the Young Academic Politician* (London: Bowes and Bowes, 1964), p. 10.

4. Kerr, *The Uses of the University,* p. 38.

5. Irving Kristol, "A Different Way to Restructure the University," *New York Times Magazine,* December 8, 1968, p. 50.

why they are in their present mess—financially and spiritually."[6]

Although both of these critics cannot be right, it is easy to find evidence to buttress either position. In support of Irving Kristol, faculties *do* seem maddeningly indifferent at times to problems that have been obvious for generations. Medical schools continue to weary first-year students with endless recitations of soon-forgotten details; many science departments still misconceive the idea of general education by forcing nonscientists to take introductory courses designed for future specialists; faculties everywhere cling to the custom of grading papers and exams without returning much in the way of comment to their students. At the same time, in defense of Jacques Barzun, one can hardly deny that colleges and universities are often distressingly inventive. Accounts of brave new ventures involving bizarre forms of experiential learning, classes on cruise ships and at ski lodges, "free" universities without grades or even formal instruction of any kind, and countless other novelties have regularly enlivened the pages of education supplements and periodicals through the years.

At the same time, sweeping generalizations like those of Kristol and Barzun fall far short of giving an adequate description of reality. Their dismissive prose seems harsh indeed for a set of educational institutions unsurpassed anywhere in the world. The negative verdicts they render on innovation are contradicted by a long list of promising initiatives that have occurred during the past generation: new schools of public policy, computer-assisted learning, advances in midcareer instruction, clinical legal education, international studies, and many more. It may be true that inertia and faddism are both represented in the history of our universities, but so is a capacity for constructive change.

Opportunities for Progress

This capacity for change will be tested over the next generation as universities come to terms with a long list of opportunities to

6. Jacques Barzun, quoted in Fred M. Hechinger, "Barzun Decries 'Service' Universities," *New York Times*, October 25, 1968, p. 50.

consider. Part of this agenda stems from initiatives now being carried on in limited or experimental form by institutions around the country. Part of it consists of unsolved problems left over from generations past. A few items are ideas just beginning to be discussed for possible action in the future. A review of these matters will serve to amplify much that I have said earlier and connect it to a larger set of concerns.

In setting their agenda, American research universities find themselves enjoying unprecedented power and influence. Never has knowledge seemed so central to our society or education so important. Never have our universities seemed so attractive not merely to young people in this country but to students all over the world and to adults of all ages. Never have universities had the opportunities that modern technology now presents to reach new audiences at work or at home through the media of video cassettes, computer programs, and televised instruction.

In making the most of these possibilities, universities must be sensitive to changes and opportunities in the world outside that bear upon their efforts to prepare students for satisfying, effective, and contributing roles in the society they will inherit. There are innumerable social trends and problems that affect academic programs in this way. To discuss these issues comprehensively and trace their implications for universities would require another book. All that can be done here is to illustrate in the simplest terms how several of the most important developments help to shape the agenda for higher education.

The first of these trends is the explosive growth of knowledge, fueled by huge investments in research and development. Henry Adams was among the first to recognize that knowledge tends to increase exponentially. The results are now imposing. More new biomedical knowledge has accumulated since the discovery of the structure of DNA in 1960 than in all of the previous generations. More books have been published since World War II than in all the preceding centuries. It took almost 275 years for Harvard to collect its first one million books and only five years to acquire its latest million.

As knowledge expands relentlessly, even specialists find it

hard to keep up in their own fields. For intellectually curious individuals, the critical problem is increasingly to figure out what to select from the accumulating mounds of books and articles in order to remain in touch, to dispel confusion, to understand important issues and formulate reasonable points of view. This problem is aggravated by the growing specialization and sophistication that mark all scientific and scholarly work and make more and more fields inaccessible to the lay mind. In the face of such quantity and complexity, those who need information must increasingly call upon mechanical means for assembling and manipulating data while relying more and more on book reviews, executive summaries, and other devices that suggest what material to read or that extract the essential information and translate it into easily digestible form.

The second prominent feature of the social environment is the continuing presence of a formidable array of national problems. Though some of these afflictions have been resolved and others have grown less severe, the total burden is not diminishing. If anything, the agenda seems more crowded and complicated than ever. Ancient dilemmas of poverty, crime, unemployment, and illiteracy appear more difficult and intractable now that so many earlier remedies have failed and we have come to appreciate how much these problems are caught up in eddies of motivation, incentive, and cultural values only dimly understood. Meanwhile, further problems have arisen, either because new groups, such as the elderly or environmentalists, have organized to press their concerns, or because fresh knowledge has uncovered hazards previously ignored, or because we have moved important functions, such as farm production and medical care, from the impersonal workings of the market economy to the conscious deliberation of policymakers in government.

To this domestic agenda has been added a host of issues resulting from the active international role the United States has pursued since World War II. As our interdependence with other parts of the world has grown, fewer and fewer important activities can be regarded any longer as purely domestic in nature.

Only rarely can a company of substantial size fail to take account of foreign markets or the threat of competition from abroad. Problems of pollution, disease, population, drugs, and many more overreach national boundaries. The vicissitudes of foreign nations and their struggles to develop economically affect our security, our economic well-being, and our daily lives, just as our policies affect theirs. Overpopulation in Mexico, austerity programs in Brazil, and meetings of oil ministers abroad have important implications for immigration into this country, the stability of our banking system, and our domestic rate of inflation. Beyond these immediate problems lies the ultimate issue of nuclear weapons, which links us to all peoples throughout the world.

The last important social development is more subjective. It expresses itself in a greater questioning of traditional values and a diminished confidence in established institutions and the credibility of their leaders. These trends are not without benefits. They have brought a richer profusion of lifestyles, a reconsideration of tired dogmas, and a public less likely to accept whatever it is told. Yet there is also no denying a certain loss of coherence and a weakening of the bonds of common belief and mutual trust that helped to bind together an earlier society and reconcile the claims of individuality and community. Contemporary culture challenges a traditional system of values that emphasized hard work, success, frugality, sexual restraint, and economic growth. Appetites fed by a consumer-oriented economy press against the Protestant ethic, casting aside the virtues of Puritanism like a "dry old Yankee stalk." Churches and schools and traditional communities no longer seem able to transmit values that society once took for granted, while mounting frustrations with an overburdened polity cause civic spirit to ebb and political apathy to grow. Amid this loosening of traditional frameworks, as Daniel Bell has observed, "the real problem of modernity is the problem of belief."[7]

7. Daniel Bell, *The Cultural Contradictions of Capitalism* (New York: Basic Books, 1976), p. 28.

Each of these several trends creates challenges for the university. The vast and rapidly growing accumulation of information and knowledge has implications at all levels of education. In the colleges, the most apparent need is to change the emphasis of instruction away from transmitting fixed bodies of information toward preparing students to engage in a continuing acquisition of knowledge and understanding. In terms of subject matter, this shift implies a greater emphasis on learning fundamental methods of intellectual inquiry and discourse and on mastering basic languages—be they foreign languages or the languages of computers and quantitative reasoning—that offer access to significant bodies of knowledge. In terms of pedagogy, the preparation for continuous learning implies a shift toward more active forms of instruction. Despite repeated changes of curriculum, most university colleges still rely on large lecture courses and extensive reading assignments that leave little room for independent thought. Too often, the result is an educational process that fails to challenge students enough to develop their powers of reasoning. This is not a happy outcome in a world where students can expect to encounter heavy demands on their intellect throughout their working lives. It is time, therefore, to think seriously about multiplying the opportunities for students to reason carefully about challenging problems under careful supervision. Such an effort will presumably call for greater emphasis on promoting active discussion in class, stronger programs to prepare instructors to teach Socratically, and increased efforts to create more thought-provoking written assignments and exams.

In many professional schools, the change in emphasis just described has long since taken place. In others, the process is far from complete. Medical schools, in particular, still rely heavily on passive lectures and extensive memorization. Fortunately, respected panels have recently issued reports calling attention to this problem, and significant changes may not be long in coming. In addition, however, medical schools, along with other professional faculties, must equip their students with techniques to cope successfully with the huge quantities of information available to them in their practice. It is a sign of the times that the experimental curriculum at the Harvard Medical School places heavy emphasis on teaching students to master the uses of the computer and to learn quantitative methods that can help them analyze complex diagnostic problems. In the future, as technology offers new capabilities for storing, sorting, and manipulating data—even to the point of giving solutions to certain types of recurring problems—no practitioner can fail to be proficient in its use.

At the postgraduate level, the rapid growth and change in the information professionals use have already done much to spur the development of midcareer education. In one field of work after another, practitioners realize that they can no longer continue indefinitely without renewing their store of knowledge. As we have discovered, these needs have now reached the point that faculties must rethink traditional practices by asking how their educational resources can best be deployed to meet the needs of individuals over their entire lifetimes. Such a reexamination is bound to require greater efforts to integrate continuing education into the regular work of the universities by acknowledging its proper claim on the attention of the faculty and on the facilities and resources of the institution. The growing importance of education to older people of all ages and the experience that these adults bring to share with faculty and students make this task all the more worthwhile.

Finally, the massive accumulation of knowledge should encourage universities to consider efforts to reach new audiences away from the campus, using new technology as well as more conventional techniques. I have already observed that the growing overload of information produces problems for even the most conscientious audience: what to read, whom to believe, how to make order out of confusion. There is much that universities can do to help. In the professions, they can use technology to permit practitioners to assess their needs and address them at home and on the job through programs of personalized instruction and self-study. Beyond the world of work, opportunities exist to help individuals educate themselves in ways important either to their personal lives or to their responsibilities as citizens. For example, there are many complicated subjects in which a university can use its expertise to guide the public through a forbidding jungle of information and argument. Communication of this kind can be of obvious value in subjects such as health, where the issues are vitally important to the public and the tangled evidence on many topics needs to be explained and evaluated by a trustworthy source. More problematic, but still worth considering, are efforts to treat more controversial subjects such as arms control, nuclear power, or primary and secondary education. In all these cases, the aim should be not to try to tell the public what to think but to help people think more effectively for themselves by making them aware of which facts are known and which are still in doubt and by clearly defining the issues and the responsible arguments on either side.

The persistence of major domestic problems presents universities with a very different challenge. If we are serious in wishing to overcome these problems, we will need the active concern and participation of a great many able and committed citizens. This fact has implications for every segment of higher education. At the undergraduate level, the liberal arts curriculum already provides much of the breadth needed to help students think seriously about important social issues. Political philosophy, economic analysis, history, sociology, and political science all offer perspectives and methods with which to explore such large questions. It is not necessary to supplement these offerings with courses specifically directed at low-income housing, welfare programs, or other domestic problems. Such material is likely to grow dated rapidly and thus fail to impart a lasting foundation of useful knowledge. What is more important is to discover ways to imbue undergraduates with a sense of commitment and civic concern that will cause them to devote their talents in later life to addressing important social problems.

Those who question this point should glance at the surveys that annually record the views and aspirations of entering college freshmen. Over the past fifteen years, the values that have risen fastest are earning lots of money, gaining positions of authority over others, and achieving recognition. The values that have slipped the most are improving race relations, helping one's community, and cleaning up the environment. These trends are disturbing; they pose a challenge to colleges to find ways of engaging more undergraduates in serious programs of community service. Fortunately, many colleges that have made this effort find that students respond with surprising enthusiasm. At Harvard, for example, over 50 percent of all undergraduates are now involved at some period in their college career in tutoring disadvantaged children, staffing centers for the homeless, visiting old-age homes, or working for some other kind of community agency. The energy and ingenuity of these undergraduates are often remarkable. One student has set up a network of projects in Third World countries to assist in rural development. Two others founded a shelter for the homeless and then persuaded the governor to donate a building which they used to create an experimental halfway house to help homeless people resume a normal life. Still others have organized groups of undergraduates to bicycle across the country each summer talking to local audiences about world hunger and raising hundreds of thousands of dollars along the way. At the least, carefully administered projects of community service can assist people in need while helping undergraduates to understand the feelings and the problems of human beings in circumstances vastly different from their own. At best, the students involved will take from their experiences an informed commitment to helping others that will carry over into their adult years and lead them to make contributions they might not otherwise have made.

The corresponding challenge for professional schools is to broaden their mission to envision a larger role for their graduates. Rather than simply train students to be competent, successful practitioners, faculties need to make greater efforts to prepare people who will look beyond their practice and strive continuously to raise the standards of the profession and improve the system in which it functions. Granted, such leadership requires qualities of character and temperament that are beyond the reach of education. Nevertheless, faculties could do much more to expand the vision of their students by encouraging them to study the history and structure of their profession and its current problems and shortcomings in meeting the legitimate needs of all segments of society. As yet, though courses of this sort exist in almost all professional schools, they seldom command the prestige or importance that goes to offerings that equip students for practice. Professors rarely make these subjects their principal fields of study, and the classes they offer typically attract only a small minority of the students. A faint aura of embarrassment often hangs over such courses, as if in apology for taking up a subject that is soft, impractical, and detached from the needs of practice in the real world. So long as this situation persists, the claim of many prominent schools to be training "leaders" of their profession will have a distressingly pretentious ring.

Beyond these efforts, a university sensitive to the problems of society should work to overcome the long-standing failure to build strong programs for students seeking careers in government and public service. Such instruction, as we have seen, presents a number of problems. Important gaps exist in our knowledge of policy analysis and public management; much of the curriculum must be invented from whole cloth; capable faculty members are in short supply; and the costs involved are often substantial. Nevertheless, enough progress has been made to suggest that universities can build programs that will attract talented students to government service and supply them with training that will be of genuine value in their professional work. At a time when the problems of state seem so vital to our welfare yet so difficult to resolve, we can no longer afford to have our educational programs for public servants lag far behind those preparing students for the major private professions.

The vast and growing importance of problems beyond our borders raises further opportunities for higher education. In particular, it underscores the need to continue the forty-year effort to internationalize our universities. With notable help from the Ford Foundation and other donors, this process has already made remarkable progress. What is called for now is continued work along a variety of fronts. In order to combat long-standing parochial and monolingual tendencies on the part of undergraduates, colleges need to persist not only in offering courses on other cultures but in searching for ways to encourage more students to spend a period of time studying or working abroad. At the same time, universities should continue to seek out more students from other nations and integrate them fully into the life of the campus community. For the next generation at least, the leading universities in this country will have an exceptional ability to attract outstanding applicants from nations around the world. Neither academic leaders nor government officials have fully appreciated what an opportunity this creates to promote greater international understanding and to help underdeveloped countries as well as to enrich the education of American students. To make the most of these possibilities, universities need to find adequate methods and resources to reach unusually talented students abroad who lack the funds or the connections to come to the United States.

As faculties respond to a student body with increasingly global interests, they will inevitably wish to strengthen their international curriculum. This trend will quickly underscore the importance of training more teachers and scholars in all international subjects. Over the last twenty years, a serious erosion has occurred in the numbers of first-rate faculty who specialize in different areas of the world or work on global problems such as economic development, international security, foreign trade, and international law. Of all the needs in international studies, this is the most crucial. No effort to make our universities more cosmopolitan will proceed very far until the problem is addressed and overcome.

The questioning of traditional values and the emergence of

many contrasting beliefs and lifestyles present an entirely different set of challenges for the university. On the one hand, if we are to remain true to our pluralistic traditions and accommodate a multitude of differing values and convictions, it is crucial to encourage undergraduates to respect contrasting attitudes and conflicting points of view. Fortunately, the American college already does well in this endeavor; one of the most pronounced effects of the undergraduate experience is to increase tolerance and weaken dogmatism. If anything, this tendency is likely to grow in the future as colleges seek increasingly diverse student bodies and stress the experience of diversity as an integral part of the educational process.

On the other hand, if universities do nothing but emphasize tolerance, they may simply succeed in fostering a kind of moral relativism that looks upon ethical questions as matters of individual preference immune from rational argument or intellectual scrutiny. Such attitudes will further weaken the ethical restraints essential to society and further loosen the bonds that join human beings together.

Such prospects call for greater efforts to search for common values and explore their contemporary meaning. This has long been the special province of the humanities. The challenge now is to renew this effort and to seek fresh syntheses that reconcile new insights and needs with more enduring human values in order to bring coherence and diversity into a healthier balance once again. The outlook for such an enterprise is especially problematic in an age when so much scholarship seems to be preoccupied with narrow specializations and abstruse theories far removed from the humane values and recurring dilemmas so long proclaimed as the focus of humanistic study. Whether the humanities can possibly live up to their traditional aspirations at a time when the surrounding culture offers so little encouragement is itself an open question. It would surely be mischievous to berate humanists for failing to succeed in an enterprise that may be beyond anyone's capacity. One can legitimately ask only that they try.

With such forbidding prospects, it is important to nurture

every promising initiative, however frail, that works to strengthen common bonds and identify common values. Even programs that encourage students to engage in community service offer a useful opportunity, for few undergraduate activities do as well in uniting a genuine cross-section of the student body in a serious effort to reach out to help and understand other people in vastly different circumstances.

Another promising development, with roots in the humanities, is the effort to present courses in moral reasoning and the analysis of ethical dilemmas in both undergraduate and professional school curricula. Properly taught, such offerings can avoid indoctrination while demonstrating that moral questions *are* susceptible to rigorous thought. Through this work, students may learn that they share more basic values than they had supposed, and that many seeming differences of opinion about ethical issues are not simply matters of conflicting personal preference but the result of hasty, poorly reasoned arguments that can be reconsidered and put aside. In these ways, courses in ethics may not only enhance a student's moral awareness but help to achieve a greater common understanding on many questions.

Once again, professors cannot give their students the character and the will to put in practice the precepts arrived at through class discussion. But even the best-intentioned individuals may not know how to respond, or even to recognize the existence of moral issues, if they have never had occasion to study recurring ethical dilemmas and consider the stock of accumulated thought on these important questions. Nor are they likely as professionals to find sufficient meaning in their work without opportunities to think through its implications for the welfare and interests of others. For all these reasons, the new courses on ethics seem promising enough that universities should regard them not as marginal electives but as basic elements of a sound education deserving of study by large segments of the student body.

Beyond the teaching of ethics, intriguing possibilities arise to strengthen the efforts in professional schools to teach the skills of human interaction. As I pointed out in an earlier chapter, professors have launched many experiments along these lines in the past fifteen years. Such initiatives deserve greater support than they have commonly received. Educating doctors to interview and counsel patients, training lawyers to negotiate, teaching businessmen to motivate their employees and colleagues are all matters that should not be left to occasional professors teaching elective courses. The skills involved are so essential to practice that every effort should be made to foster such instruction and extend it to all students. In doing so, however, professional schools need to make these offerings more than simply a means of providing tools for effective practice. Just as instruction in ethics can degenerate into indoctrination, so can the teaching of negotiation or counseling become an exercise in manipulation. Such teaching is not only destructive but misleading and superficial as well. For example, it is naive and self-defeating to think that successful negotiation consists in finding clever ways to take advantage of other people. At their best, all of the skills of human interaction require insight into the feelings and needs of others and a search for some basis of mutual benefit and satisfaction. For this reason, such instruction offers an opportunity not only to prepare students for practice but to encourage them to work in many small ways to rebuild the sense of community, trust, and credibility that seems to have receded so markedly in modern society.

A Better Environment for Learning

In constructing their agenda, universities must avoid the temptation to focus only on adding courses and reorganizing programs. To do so would simply reinforce the common tendency to emphasize what faculties teach and to ignore how students learn. Such oversight would be unfortunate. Important as they are, the new courses and programs I have described will make up only a small fraction of the curriculum. But other opportunities exist to enhance the quality of student learning, opportunities that can benefit all academic programs at all levels in the university.

Of particular importance is the creation of an environment

that rewards and encourages better teaching. Building such an environment is not a matter of one dramatic initiative. It requires a variety of incentives and rewards to complement the recognition and prestige that already come to excellence in research. One of these incentives surely involves paying serious attention to the quality of teaching, in addition to research, in deciding on appointments and promotions. Another is to encourage careful, systematic student evaluation of courses that will help instructors discover areas in which their teaching and course materials need improvement. A third is to offer grants to faculty members wishing to make their courses better or to experiment with new methods of instruction. Such support will be especially important in encouraging new uses of computer technology that can help students learn more effectively. A fourth step is to assist young professors and graduate students to develop their teaching skills. Such help can come through written materials, colloquia, or seminars or, better still, through the use of videotape that allows instructors to watch themselves in the act of teaching and to discuss their performance with an experienced critic. Together, these four initiatives and others like them can build greater concern for the quality of teaching while helping those who wish to improve.

Strengthening the environment for learning involves more than encouraging individual instructors. There are useful initiatives that faculties need to work at collaboratively. Among them are the basic steps I described in discussing the state of undergraduate education: agreeing on the aims of each program, explaining these purposes to students, considering how to adapt courses and exams to further the common goals, and providing careful assessment to inform students of their intellectual progress. Beyond these efforts lie more difficult and challenging questions such as how to develop critical thinking or nurture a capacity for creativity and imagination.

Another important step toward enhancing learning is a commitment to help students who perform below their capacity. Every university has many candidates for such assistance. They enroll in the most selective institutions just as in programs with open admissions. They populate professional schools as well as colleges.

Universities can assist such students in many ways—by teaching them to read more rapidly or to study more effectively or by referring them for counseling if they have psychological difficulties. A well-developed effort, however, will not merely help floundering students to adjust; it will also serve as a valuable resource for informing the faculty of pervasive student problems that call for changes in the academic program itself. Gentle prodding may remind universities that they are often less sensitive than they should be to the varying learning needs of different groups of students. For example, instead of trying to bring every student to a reasonable level of achievement by adjusting the time and instruction provided to complete a body of work, universities are inclined to give everyone the same amount of time and attention and then grade down the students who fall behind. This practice can be cruelly wasteful of human talent. As one recent study points out: "It has become evident that a large portion of slower learners can learn to the same achievement level as the faster learners. When the slower learners do succeed in attaining the same criterion of achievement as the faster learners, they appear to be able to learn equally complex and abstract ideas, they can apply these ideas to new problems, and they can retain the ideas equally well in spite of the fact that they learned with more time and help than was given to others."[8] Clearly, much work is needed to determine how best to assist students and whether it is feasible to provide all the help required. Too often, especially in graduate and professional schools, such efforts are simply not made.

One final challenge underlies all the others. Efforts to improve learning cannot progress very far, except by chance, unless universities find some method of determining which initiatives succeed and which do not. Professors are less likely to

8. Benjamin S. Bloom, George F. Madaus, and J. Thomas Hastings, *Evaluation to Improve Learning* (New York: McGraw-Hill, 1981), p. 60.

experiment with new methods of instruction or to adopt the innovations of others if they have no way of knowing what educational gains will result. Hence, universities need to make a sustained effort to investigate the process of teaching and learning and to evaluate its effects on students. Deans and other academic leaders should help organize such research and direct it to issues that will aid faculty members and administrators in making sounder choices about instructional methods, the use of technology, the forms of examination, the size of classes, and other options within their control. Because such questions are often hard to explore, this work will not always yield immediate returns. Nevertheless, studies can be carried out even now that will throw valuable light on many concrete decisions educators are called upon to make. In time, continued work should succeed in expanding this list considerably.

The Process of Educational Reform

The agenda just described is a long one. No single university can expect to push forward on every front at once. But it is reasonable to ask whether we can expect universities to address at least some of these needs over the next decade. How might the process of reform move forward? What obstacles might get in the way?

Universities are large, decentralized, informal organizations with little hierarchical authority over teaching and research. These characteristics favor innovation by making it easy for any of a large number of faculty members to experiment in search of better ways of educating students. Unfortunately, the very factors that aid experimentation make it harder for successful initiatives to spread throughout the institution or from one institution to another. Since academic administrators do not have the power to insist that faculties adopt new techniques, new courses, or new curricula, the most promising innovations can easily languish unless some effective force causes them to be emulated widely.

Of course, promising experiments may spread simply by virtue of a desire to improve the quality of education. Faculty members and administrators do pay attention to reports of programs and initiatives established at sister institutions. They often copy experiments tried elsewhere, especially those which seem to address a common problem successfully or attract a new student audience.

Of the many proposals listed at the beginning of this chapter, a few are likely to spread through emulation of this kind. Computer use may grow, if only because universities that fail to adopt successful applications will seem old-fashioned to their students and faculty. If professional schools for public service are successful, other universities will add them as donors begin to show interest and as the programs become a source of intellectual interest to faculty members. Executive courses for established professionals will surely continue to multiply, if only because their constituents will press for them and can usually pay for the costs.

The Role of Competition

Despite these possibilities, in the busy environment of the research university, the desire to innovate and improve is often not strong enough to overcome inertia and to ensure a determined, systematic effort to enhance the quality of education. In other walks of life, competition is frequently the mechanism that drives individuals and organizations to surmount such inhibitions and to strive continuously to improve. But competition succeeds only to the extent that customers, judges, or other trusted sources can define success in some legitimate way in order to establish a standard and reward those who best achieve it. In education, at least at the university level, this ability is lacking. Neither students nor other interested audiences can tell how effective their education is or how its quality compares with that of other universities.

One reason for this ignorance is a lack of clarity over the ends being pursued. Most professors and students can state in general terms the principal aims of a college or professional school education. But agreement breaks down when one tries to specify exactly which skills, bodies of knowledge, or methods of thought are deemed important by the faculty. As a result, students cannot always compare what they are likely to learn at different institutions.

More important than the confusion over goals is the problem of finding out how successful universities are in helping their students attain these ends. On this score, ignorance reigns. No universities attempt to measure the amount their students learn, let alone compare the results with those of rival institutions. As a result, applicants have little information to help them decide at which college or professional school they are likely to learn the most.

Lacking such information, students pick their college and professional school on a variety of other grounds. Geography is obviously a potent consideration, judging by the large proportions of young people who attend institutions within fifty miles of their homes. Some students will choose a university because it offers a particular program of special interest, or because it is denominational in character, or because close friends and relatives are already enrolled. For those with intellectual interests or ambitions for a professional career, other criteria usually prove decisive. Typically, such students look for institutions that seem most likely to engage their interests and to assist them in their later lives. These concerns lead them to pay particular attention to institutional prestige, a vague amalgam made up of the scholarly reputation of the faculty, the quality of the student body, and the success of graduates in finding good jobs and being accepted at leading professional schools.

Defined in this way, prestige is not a trivial basis for choosing a college or professional school. A faculty highly respected for its scholarly work is likely to have more to teach than a faculty that publishes little. Since students often learn much from one another, the quality of the student body is also a valid consideration. The problem is not that students are irrational or frivolous in making their selections. The point is simply that student choices based on institutional prestige do not exert much pressure on colleges and professional schools to take specific steps to improve the quality of their education. On the contrary, a university with a faculty of high renown and a reputation for selective admissions can continue to attract able students even if it makes no special effort along these lines.

Students do exert some influence, albeit a limited one, on the quality of education. Within groups of universities that enjoy comparable prestige, applicants may strongly prefer certain policies or practices offered by only some of the members. By flocking to universities that follow these policies, they can exert much pressure on the remaining institutions to follow suit. For example, the marked preference for coeducation on the part of students in the 1960s eventually forced all Ivy League universities to open their doors to women. Even within a single college or professional school, departments and individual instructors often feel substantial pressure to offer courses attractive enough to keep their enrollments from falling.

The pressures created in this way will actually improve the quality of learning only to the extent that students can identify better education and insist upon it in choosing a school to attend. On this score, the evidence is mixed. Students can certainly recognize palpable shoddiness and neglect, so that universities cannot allow such conditions to exist without serious risk of losing applicants. But there is no convincing evidence that students are capable of making sound choices where subtler questions are involved. Findings are mixed on whether undergraduates perform better on examinations in classes where they like the professor or enjoy the methods of instruction used. A few investigations even suggest that the reverse may be true. Experience offers little basis for supposing that students will press for educational improvements provided the current state of teaching is reasonably adequate. Indeed, students are often rather conservative when professors seek to abandon familiar methods and try something new, especially if workloads rise as a result. All in all, therefore, the students' ability to "vote with their feet" appears to be too crude an instrument to bring about any sustained pressure for increasing the effectiveness of teaching and learning.

Another competitive force that could conceivably help to improve the quality of education comes from employers. In principle, those who hire university graduates could put pressure on colleges and professional schools by preferring applicants who have taken programs that closely correspond to employers' perceptions of what one needs to know to perform effectively. For example, law firms might favor graduates of schools that make special efforts to teach not only the process of legal reasoning but the practical arts of negotiation, litigation, and interviewing witnesses as well. If enough firms followed such a hiring policy, students would move to the favored schools, and other institutions would soon have to adjust their curricula accordingly. But neither law firms nor other types of employers seem ready to proceed on this basis. In the end, they prefer to look for students of intellectual talent without much regard to the courses they have taken or the skills they purport to have learned.

Despite the keen rivalry in attracting students, then, the effects of competition on the quality of education are weaker and more haphazard than they are in the commercial world or in many other fields of endeavor. On the positive side, the rivalry that exists among colleges and universities seems to encourage more innovation in teaching methods, better services and facilities for students, and greater variety to meet the differing tastes and aptitudes of potential applicants. The effects of competition on the curriculum are more ambiguous, not because universities fail to adapt to the desires of their students but because educators question the ability of students to know the kind of education they really need. In addition, because it is so hard for anyone to know how effective universities are in helping students learn, competition does not serve to drive out institutions of poor quality. Nor does it do much, as I have just pointed out, to encourage faculty members and administrators to work continuously to enhance the quality of education.

The gains achieved from competition may be further weakened in research universities by another aspect of the rivalry among institutions. Everyone would acknowledge that the pressures and rewards of competition are much, much greater in carrying on research and in trying to build the reputation of the faculty than they are in education (in large part because the results of research are more credibly and more frequently evaluated and compared). The effect is to draw energy away from education to research, since it is only natural to work hardest at activities that are most commonly judged by one's peers and most handsomely rewarded by one's profession. Of course, teaching and scholarship do not constitute a "zero-sum game." Efforts to encourage research and to improve the scholarly reputation of the faculty may enhance the quality of education by producing a faculty with more ideas and knowledge to impart to students. But competition undoubtedly makes it harder to mount a sustained, systematic effort within the faculty to achieve the kinds of educational change described earlier in this chapter.

External Pressure

Competition is not the only means of exerting influence from outside to bring about widespread educational reform. As we have discovered, other forces in the external world can have important effects on teaching programs. The development of computers affords one example; the growing demand in many professions for midcareer instruction offers another.

There are also more deliberate efforts from outside to improve the quality of education. For example, private accrediting bodies send teams to visit universities periodically. Although their primary task is to enforce minimum standards, they ask all institutions in advance of their visit to carry out a process of self-study that can help to focus energies for reform. They also make suggestions for change even to institutions that are clearly in no danger of losing their accreditation. Although these efforts are useful, reviews take place only once in several years, and there is no way to guarantee that faculties whose accreditation is secure will cooperate fully in scrutinizing their own performance. Overall, therefore, accreditation is an imperfect instrument to ensure reasonable quality, let alone to bring about the kinds of improvements described earlier in this chapter.

A different type of outside pressure is the force of informed opinion. Not all criticism, of course, has an appreciable impact. But occasionally a thoughtful critique is remarkably effective in bringing about reform. For example, the Flexner Report of 1910 castigated proprietary schools of medicine, helping to hasten their demise, and recommended a science-based curriculum that medical schools in universities quickly adopted. Similarly, the publication in 1958 of two lengthy reports on business education sponsored by the Ford and Carnegie foundations led many colleges and business schools to improve their programs by cutting back descriptive courses, emphasizing economics, statistics, and other rigorous disciplines, and strengthening programs of research. More recently, national reports on the state of undergraduate education have helped to persuade more than half of our colleges to review their academic programs or to make plans for doing so in the future.

A closer look at the Flexner, Ford, and Carnegie reports reveals why these particular documents were so successful. In each case the final report recommended changes that were already under way, changes that would achieve higher academic standards of a traditional kind. Although the suggestions were not original, the three reports helped to speed reform by mobilizing informed opinion and building a climate supportive of change. Yet the progress that resulted would hardly have occurred had the recommendations not conformed to values already widely held within many faculties. In support of this point, one need only look to portions of the Flexner report that did *not* have significant influence: suggestions that medical schools should teach the social and preventive dimensions of health, or cut back the number of lectures. The latter ideas were largely ignored. Their failing was not that they were ill-considered, but merely that they fell outside prevailing beliefs in leading medical schools about what was important in medical education.

Aside from criticism, the principal outside influence for reform is the award of funds to support new initiatives. This method has been used repeatedly and to good effect. Companies have offered large subsidies that have helped persuade universities to invest heavily in computers. Ford Foundation grants played an important role in the development of law school clinical programs. And government agencies have frequently offered grants as a means of inducing medical schools to develop new training programs or expand old ones to meet growing needs in the society.

Despite these successes, external granting agencies play only a limited role in enhancing the quality of education. Very rarely will a foundation or a government agency display any interest in trying to strengthen universities in carrying out their regular functions. Instead, the common tendency is to look upon them as helpful instruments to use in trying to attack some pressing problem in the outside world such as arms control, cancer, poverty, or mental health. Next to these endeavors, efforts to improve the quality of instruction or inquire into the effectiveness of educational programs seem tame. Besides, proposals to fund work of this kind are difficult to evaluate and their results even harder to assess. The net result, therefore, is to regard such undertakings as matters that institutions should finance for themselves, like renovations in the faculty club or acquisitions for the library.

In sum, then, influences from outside the campus have a positive but limited effect on teaching and education. Criticism can attract attention and reorder priorities, while money often facilitates experimentation. Such pressures are frequently helpful, sometimes even essential. They are most useful when they echo thoughts already present in the faculty and strengthen the hand of educators who wish to bring these ideas to fruition. But no external influence offers a reliable way of initiating constructive change or eliciting new ideas to improve the quality of education. This vital task ultimately rests within the university itself.

The Role of the Faculty

Rarely can improvements in education occur without the active cooperation of the faculty. It is the professors who teach the courses and who have the erudition to convey something valuable to their students. At their best, they offer compelling examples of what it means to have an educated mind, to love a subject, to think deeply about a problem. Margaret Mead's recollections of Franz Boas, Walter Lippmann's account of conversations with William James, and countless other remembrances suggest that personal examples of this kind often leave a more lasting imprint than any calculated effort to improve the quality of teaching.

Collectively, however, faculties often seem distressingly sluggish and unwilling to change. Problems first noted fifty or even one hundred years ago still persist in colleges and professional schools. Examining this record, many critics ascribe the slow pace of reform to indifference or willful neglect. This diagnosis is not entirely fair. Professors have other interests that compete with teaching, but few would have entered academic life had they not been genuinely interested in teaching and in the welfare of their students. The greatest obstacles to change lie elsewhere.

A common impediment is the inability to understand certain subjects well enough to teach them effectively. As we have seen, this was a major reason why it took so long to develop a challenging curriculum to prepare students for public service. It has also been an important factor in keeping professional schools from doing more to develop the skills of human relations or to foster such traits as creativity and imagination among their students.

In considering new fields of instruction, universities are also blocked at times by a lack of competent professors. The teaching of applied ethics has clearly encountered this problem. Clinical legal programs have likewise suffered from a dearth of faculty members who can teach the necessary skills effectively and can also write perceptively enough to satisfy their more traditional colleagues. Similar frustrations have impeded efforts to assemble strong faculties to prepare students for careers in public service.

Further barriers to change arise when reforms threaten important academic values, particularly the primacy of intellectual standards. The principal reason college faculties have often balked at awarding academic credit for dance, painting, or musical performance is not that professors disdain the arts but that artistic performance does not call for the exercise of intellectual qualities that can be evaluated in traditional ways. Similarly, we have seen that law professors sometimes resist integrating clinical programs into the regular curriculum because many instructors in these programs do not carry on research of the usual kind. While these objections may seem petty at first glance, they conceal more substantial reservations. Professors in many colleges fear that unless undergraduates must meet some credible standard of achievement, giving academic credit will run the risk of trivializing the educational experience and losing the respect of serious students. Law faculties believe that unless they insist that prospective colleagues do serious research, they risk appointing professors who will fail to renew their intellectual capital and will eventually grow stale and ineffective in the classroom. One may argue that faculties could show more imagination in overcoming these problems, but one cannot simply ascribe their behavior to laziness or to a congenital reluctance to change.

Not surprisingly, innovations also face rough sledding if they demand large amounts of time and effort on the part of the faculty or divert money and resources from traditional uses. Most professors in research universities are forever busy, and funds seem always in short supply. Of course, few professors will resist a reform, however burdensome, if they are genuinely convinced that it will aid the intellectual growth of their students. But the results of educational reform are rarely clear enough to meet this test. Once again, the lack of trusted methods of evaluation takes its toll on the willingness to change.

Finally, faculties will resist new initiatives that are so large or so visible that failure could diminish the prestige of the institution or impair its ability to attract able students and talented professors. This inhibition seriously affects the likelihood of major reforms. Since leading schools enjoy the best students and faculty, they have the most to lose by gambling on large innovations. (Their professors are also likely to be the most preoccupied with research and hence least able to find the time to carry out major institutional reforms.) Thus, the schools that have the greatest chance of influencing other institutions through successful innovation are the ones least inclined to be venturesome. To them, there is much wisdom in Cornford's observation that "nothing should ever be done for the first time."[9] Such caution helps to explain why so many ambitious experiments occur in lesser-known universities, such as McMasters and New Mexico in the field of medical education or Northeastern in law. This tendency would not matter much in a truly competitive environment. In education, however, competitive pressures are sufficiently weak that smaller schools sometimes make very successful innovations only to see them languish and produce no effect on other institutions.

The obstacles and inhibitions just described do not block educational progress altogether, but they do have a telling effect on what kinds of changes occur and how they come about. The most numerous and successful changes are those that further the professional interests and values of the faculty and do not cost exorbitant amounts of money. The new ideas and fresh insights constantly added to traditional courses, the steady introduction of new subjects, the gradual changes in the intellectual demands teachers make on students, all exemplify this type of gradual reform. The process typically resembles the growth of a coral reef more than the eruption of a volcano. Only rarely do the changes come rapidly, as they did in the wake of the Flexner report on medical schools and the Carnegie and Ford studies on business education. Yet the results of this constant accretion are impressive. One study of 110 colleges in the 1960s revealed that

9. Cornford, *Microcosmographia Academica*, p. 23.

over a five-year period a full 20 percent of all courses were replaced or reorganized, while new offerings were added at an average rate of 9 percent per year.[10] For some kinds of change, no other process will be effective. For example, if the humanities are indeed in a state of crisis, they will emerge from it only through the work of many individual professors and not by any planned reform.

Another means of securing important changes is to proceed outside the existing systems of formal instruction and thus avoid the need for faculty approval. The outlook for such changes is much more favorable. One need only assemble willing participants and provide them with the resources to proceed; no sacrifices are required of the faculty as a whole. These advantages help to explain why at the undergraduate level extracurricular activities and student services have grown so much more rapidly than innovative teaching methods. The same reasons account for the fact that programs in public policy have developed much faster when they have been established as separate schools than when they have had to compete for resources within existing faculties of business administration.

Programs in the arts illustrate the limits of this method of achieving progress. Most of these activities begin outside the formal curriculum—or at any rate their demands on the curriculum are limited and their claims on the time and resources of the regular faculty even less substantial. As long as the new programs remain in this peripheral status, they flourish without much restraint, despite their unconventional ways. Eventually, however, instructors in the arts often ask for faculty status and seek more resources as well as academic credit for student participants. At this point, the pace of reform will often slow as members of the faculty start to criticize the programs for lacking rigor and intellectual content.

A closely related means of instituting change within the curriculum is to proceed on an experimental basis. This tactic has

10. J. B. Lon Hefferlin, *Dynamics of Academic Reform* (San Francisco: Jossey-Bass, 1969), pp. 54–58.

obvious advantages. It relies entirely on volunteers and hence makes few, if any, demands on unwilling faculty members. It costs less than an institution-wide reform. It minimizes the risks of failure by leaving traditional programs intact. These virtues are often decisive in holding open the chance of making a substantial change. For example, Harvard Medical School has recently undertaken a major initiative to reform medical education by radically reducing the number of lectures, emphasizing the use of computers and modern decisionmaking techniques, and introducing more work on ethics, health economics, and the psychological and social aspects of medicine. Persuading the entire faculty to adopt the new curriculum and to alter their methods of teaching was out of the question. With strong support from the dean, however, and from a group of enthusiastic faculty participants, the project was approved on an experimental basis for a small number of students.

The problem in such a case is how to spread an innovation through the entire institution once it seems to have succeeded. The ideal course would be to evaluate the new venture objectively and appeal to the professional standards of the faculty by demonstrating that it produces superior educational results. As we have seen, however, methods of evaluation are often too primitive to give this strategy much chance of success. The measures are almost always imperfect, and skeptics can quickly find reasons to explain why students who are showered with attention in an experimental program perform better than their peers in traditional classes.

The reformer's hope, therefore, is that the new venture will be successful enough to overcome all opposition. It may prove to be so popular that other students will insist on having it too. If conservative faculty members see that they can adopt the new methods without excessive risk or trouble, they may gradually come around to accepting the innovation. Something of this kind seems to be occurring at many universities in the use of computers to supplement regular instruction. As more students enroll already knowing how to use computers and a few professors demonstrate the uses of these machines, students begin to ask other instructors why they too cannot employ the new technology. If adequate funds and support services become available, more and more professors may start to experiment with computer applications of their own. Alas, not all deserving experiments will succeed in this fashion. Some of them may not arouse student interest; others may not attract outside support; still others will entail so much work that they will be left to die a quiet death. Nevertheless, experiments have given life to many lasting innovations that would not otherwise have gotten under way.

In light of this list of inhibitions and possibilities, what can faculties do on their own to address the major educational challenges facing universities? They will certainly continue to incorporate new knowledge into their teaching and to take advantage of new technologies that are not too burdensome or expensive to use. They will undoubtedly continue to add new courses and even introduce new programs and new majors. A few venturesome instructors will find imaginative uses for computers in the classrooms and will experiment with new ways of teaching important professional skills or new courses in ethics and social responsibility. If foundations and other outside funding sources provide support, the pace of such experimentation not only will be sustained but may quicken appreciably.

Today, however, what universities need most is not simply continued experimentation or a gradual incorporation of new courses and new knowledge. These processes are already going on with considerable vigor. What is more important now is a determined effort to evaluate new initiatives and to move the successful ones into the mainstream of the curriculum where they can have greater permanence and reach more students.

There appear to be no absolute barriers to carrying out such reforms. All of them can begin without waiting for new technological discoveries or new advances in knowledge (although such advances would often be helpful). None of these ventures is so prominent as to risk the reputation of an institution, with the possible exception of a new school of public policy. Although substantial sums may be needed for some of the initiatives, such as computer applications or larger enrollments of foreign students, most of the changes will require only modest resources.

The greatest resistance is likely to come from faculty members who fear that the proposals will take time to implement and thus diminish their opportunities for research. If something has to give, they will urge, let it be teaching, not because teaching is unimportant but because research is more important and may even improve the content, if not the execution, of the educational program.

There are many answers to this argument. For one thing, few of the proposals I have made will require much time of the faculty, at least the great majority of the faculty. For another, there are many ways to compensate for lost time by reducing the effort that professors have to spend on tasks that are not as important as *either* education or research. Another problem with this line of argument is that it is based on a questionable belief similar to the conviction of many students that the more time they spend on their studies the better they will do academically. Such claims are not well supported by evidence. It is not simply the amount of time but the quality and intensity of the effort that determine the success achieved. Thus, investigations of several kinds of human endeavor suggest that busy people with many claims on their time often accomplish more than those single-mindedly devoted to one activity. Of course, this does not mean that scientists and scholars can devote any amount of effort to improving education without impairing the quality of their research. It does suggest that faculty members could make the limited commitment needed to help carry out the changes I have been discussing without much risk to their scholarly work.

Even if professors have time for the task, most of these initiatives are not ones that faculties are likely to carry out alone. In some cases, new ventures will die for lack of spontaneous interest. Without constant encouragement, for example, few instructors will be inclined to make much of an effort to teach practical skills or professional ethics, or work with underachieving students, or carry out research to evaluate their own teaching. Other changes call for actions that faculties are not in a good position to take even if they wish to do so. A group of professors may have a latent interest in educating students for public service, but they can hardly be expected to raise the money and build the facilities needed to bring such a program into being. Nor are they well equipped to create centers to improve teaching, or arrange large-scale uses of computers, or develop programs for practitioners in midcareer. The same is true of organizing major efforts to help underachieving students, to carry out research on teaching, to increase the number of foreign students, or indeed, to create any other program that requires funds, organizational talents, new buildings, and other resources beyond the reach of ordinary faculty members.

The Role of the Administration

What emerges from this discussion is that the reforms most needed in higher education are unlikely to occur automatically from the effects of competition, or from the initiatives of foundations and government agencies, or from the spontaneous efforts of professors. While few important changes can occur without faculty support, something more is required in the form of entrepreneurial skill in order to bring about major educational reforms. Deans, provosts and, ultimately, presidents are the obvious candidates to supply this added impetus.

American higher education has traditionally produced leadership of this kind. Behind every college erected in the eighteenth and nineteenth centuries was a resolute founding figure armed with unusual qualities of resourcefulness and tenacity. Strong presidents toward the beginning of the twentieth century were chiefly responsible for creating the large research-oriented universities we know today, guiding their institutions successfully through an era of even greater change than higher education is currently experiencing.

Is it still possible for academic leaders to bring about significant change? As we have seen, many observers seem to doubt it. According to these critics, whatever power exists in the academy has shifted from presidents into the hands of the faculty. Professors are the central force in the modern university; their distinction shapes the reputation of the institution, and their contributions are essential to its success. Now that they have secured lifetime tenure, now that they contribute more than presidents do to enhance the university's prestige, now that they earn much of their salary from the government rather than their university, they need not accept direction from any president or dean. They and they alone decide what to teach, whom to teach, and when to teach. Presidents can explain the faculty's actions to the outside world; they can raise money, build new buildings, and defend the institution from hostile attacks; but they lack the authority to bring about serious educational reform.

No one can deny the general drift of the argument. Faculties have doubtless gained power in this century relative to presidents and deans. Gone are the days when President Wheeler could gallop across the Berkeley campus on a white horse and President Eliot could appoint Harvard professors with scarcely any consultation with the faculty. Still, it may be too soon to write off the luckless administrators. Even today, they possess attributes and powers that put them in a unique position to foster educational reform.

To begin with, academic leaders can have a much greater incentive than the average faculty member to bring about significant changes. Unlike professors, presidents and deans have reason to believe that educational reform still ranks high among the achievements by which their tenure will be judged. If they understand this and care about education, the resulting motivation will be an important asset in an environment where innovation encounters such inertia and where so much patience and perseverance are required to make it spread and take root.

For all the talk about the loss of authority to the faculty, academic leaders also retain several powers of substantial importance. Typically, they have a unique opportunity to raise funds as well as the authority to allocate resources (at least at the margin) and, in many universities, to veto faculty appointments. These powers may not command obedience—and a good thing, too. But most presidents and deans have enough authority to guarantee them an attentive audience. If they cannot force agreement, they can at least make proposals and expect to have them carefully considered.

In part because of their unique perspective and in part because of the authority of their office, academic leaders also have a special opportunity to mobilize support for new initiatives. If anyone is to have a vision for a university and communicate its basic directions and priorities, that person is likely to be a president or some other official with broad academic responsibilities. It is easy to be cynical about the influence such individuals actually wield, especially over the faculty. But most professors, like everyone else, are not totally committed to a fixed intellectual agenda. They too have time at the margin. They too have secret doubts about how much of what they do really matters. It is this residuum of flexibility and uncertainty that gives to presidents and deans the chance to use their persuasive powers to create new priorities and mobilize faculty energies behind them.

The authority retained by presidents and deans enables them not only to shape the academic agenda but to create an environment that promotes innovation and develops support for new ideas. With their power to allocate resources among different activities and programs in the university, they can create incentives to support experimentation and encourage greater attention to teaching and education. They can offer funds to professors wishing to try new methods; they can make available expensive equipment, such as computers; they can persuade influential faculty members to try out promising initiatives; they can find ways of rewarding and recognizing those who contribute most to educational change. To supplement these material incentives, they also have the ability to mobilize information to promote reform. They can create a committee of outside experts to review programs and recommend change, or institute student evaluations of courses and thereby mobilize opinion against ineffective teachers, or collect data to document the strengths of certain programs and the weaknesses of others.

Finally, presidents and deans have special capacities to implement new initiatives. Once the decision is made to found a new professional school for public service, a new series of midcareer programs, a center for improving the quality of teaching, or an innovative curriculum in a college or professional school, the support of the academic leadership becomes crucial. Only rarely can anyone other than a president or dean raise the funds, recruit the staff, and find the facilities needed to bring these projects to fruition.

Of course, it is one thing to have such powers and quite another to use them effectively. As many writers have pointed out, presidents no longer have the time to play an informed, effective role in educational policy even if they have the power to do so. A century ago, the scholarly world was still sufficiently limited and universities were still small enough that a strong academic leader could try to keep up with most of the academic fields within his institution. That era has long since passed. Knowledge has grown so specialized and complicated that no one person can hope to keep abreast of the intellectual currents in more than a few of the many disciplines and professional schools. Uninformed about so many fields of learning, presidents cannot readily learn where the opportunities are, let alone determine how to exploit them. In addition, academic institutions today are much larger and the methods of administering them more complex. Many groups, from the federal government to the local community, are interested in the behavior of the university. All these groups clamor for attention and ask to participate in the decisions that affect them. Meanwhile, the burdens of fundraising have grown gargantuan, a web of federal regulations has descended on the campus, and the problems of personnel, budgeting, facilities planning, debt management, and other administrative tasks have increased several-fold. In this environment, presidents and other administrators work harder and harder and still find less and less time to spend on serious educational issues.

These difficulties account for the greatest paradox currently facing university presidents and deans (along with those who direct hospitals, museums, and most other large nonprofit institutions). Such officials are typically drawn from academic life and lack formal training or extensive experience in administration. They are chosen despite these handicaps because most people agree that leaders of educational institutions need to understand the principal values and concerns of the academy in order to give wise, long-term direction. And yet, the irony is that academic leaders have less and less time to give to the intellectual agenda they were chosen to pursue. Instead, they must devote almost all their energies to the very administrative tasks for which they are so notably unprepared.

This situation poses dangers for the vitality of our universities. If nothing is done to address the problem, one of two things will happen. Trustees may select as presidents individuals known chiefly for their managerial and political skills rather than their intellectual qualities. In this event, presidents will have little academic leadership to give to their institutions. To avoid this problem, governing boards may turn to scholars who lack experience with the financial and managerial issues that confront them. The consequence of this strategy will be to force presidents to devote so much time to mastering these administrative duties that they have no chance to think about academic questions. Either way, the progress of education in the university will suffer.

It is not easy to know how to escape from this predicament. Some institutions, such as the Metropolitan Museum in New York, have tried a dual system of leadership, with separate intellectual and administrative heads. Under this arrangement, exhibitions and acquisitions are left to the artistic director while the chief administrator worries about raising money, maintaining the buildings, balancing the books, and dealing with the community. A similar arrangement could be made to divide the academic and managerial responsibilities of the university. In practice, however, it is difficult to separate these functions, since intellectual aims condition the choice of management policies while administrative decisions impinge upon the intellectual life of the institution. Hence, a dual system can work only so long as the two leaders have the patience and understanding to work in harmony together. Such a relationship certainly cannot be counted upon indefinitely.

Another possibility is to rely on provosts and deans to provide academic leadership while the president represents the university to the outside world and oversees its administrative and support systems. This scheme may work. But success depends on making sure that the deans and provosts are not overloaded with petty administrative and fundraising responsibilities so that they too are forced to neglect the larger educational issues. Even if they are given sufficient authority, they may still lack the capacity for educational leadership unless they are carefully chosen with that end in mind. Unfortunately, presidents who devote their energies chiefly to fundraising and administration are not likely to make inspired choices or even to work very hard at finding gifted deans. Instead, they will often delegate the power of selection to search committees or entire faculties. As a result, those appointed will not represent the president's choice to achieve a set of educational goals and may simply be compromise candidates selected to maintain a comfortable status quo. In such a situation, gifted deans will emerge now and then, but the record is bound to be spotty, and the direction of the university as a whole can hardly hope to be consistent.

Perhaps the best approach would be to preserve a unitary presidency held by someone with a strong academic background while delegating more authority over management to a treasurer or executive vice president with truly impressive administrative experience. The aim would be to have a strong enough administrative and financial team that presidents need not concern themselves with such matters except for occasional issues of broad policy or questions with a direct bearing on academic interests. Even this arrangement could leave presidents with a hefty fundraising and ceremonial burden. But they could have at least a chance of finding enough time left over to pay attention to the educational direction of the institution.

Whatever the answer, presidents and trustees should think hard about how to create the conditions that will make educational leadership possible on their campuses. Although it is fashionable to slight the role of the administration and to emphasize the power of the faculty, the truth is that neither can accomplish much reform without the other. By themselves, faculties can offer new courses or package familiar offerings to create new programs. Administrators can fund new professorships, build new buildings, or add new services. All these steps are important. Together, they constitute most of the change that typically occurs in universities. But none of them will suffice to capitalize on the most important opportunities currently before us to improve the quality of education. For that to occur, cooperation between strong leadership *and* a willing faculty is indispensable.

This account of how education changes leaves us with a final question. Is there any way to ensure that universities will do their utmost to meet their new challenges and satisfy the needs of students and society? There are two familiar methods in this country for trying to keep human organizations attentive to the public interest. One is regulation; the other, competition. The problem is that neither seems quite apt for our purposes. Government regulation and control have not worked well to improve the quality of education—not for American public schools and not for universities abroad. But, as we have seen, competition does not work perfectly either. Although it produces much diversity, experimentation, and creative adaptation, it does not bring about an ideal curriculum, it does not effectively eliminate institutions of poor quality, and it does not force institutions to work systematically to enhance the learning of their students.

While each of the familiar methods of control falls short of the ideal, there is little doubt which of them works best. Nothing in the experience of our public schools and nothing we can discover overseas suggests that stronger government regulation will significantly improve the processes of teaching and learning in our colleges and universities. On the contrary, government intervention would threaten important qualities of venturesomeness and diversity that have flourished under our competitive, decentralized system. Hence, whatever improvements can be made are most likely to result not from strengthening the hand of government but from finding ways to improve the functioning of the free, autonomous system we already have.

One possibility is to strengthen the process of accreditation by toughening standards and asking institutions to examine the efforts they are making to enhance the quality of teaching and learning. This shift in emphasis would doubtless cause universities to pay more attention to the process of education. Yet we must not exaggerate the prospects. Accreditation will have its principal effect on a small number of marginal institutions and will exert much less influence on the large majority of colleges and universities whose status is secure. Even with marginal institutions, political and practical restraints severely limit the power to raise standards and withdraw accreditation. There is little reason to expect these inhibitions to diminish in the future.

Another possibility is to make more useful information available to students to help them reach more enlightened decisions about what college or professional school to attend. For example, the government could require each institution to disclose such matters as the aims of its educational programs, the qualifications of the faculty, the composition and achievements of the student body, and the size and nature of the library, laboratory, and other facilities. With help from foundations, efforts could also be made to improve upon the guides that currently evaluate colleges and professional schools for the benefit of prospective applicants. By helping students to choose more wisely, assistance of this kind could put constructive pressure on colleges and universities to improve themselves in order to achieve a higher rating.

While these measures are worth considering, the foreseeable gains, once again, seem limited. If we could measure how much students progress toward important educational goals, we could offer applicants a sound basis for deciding which institutions might benefit them most. By influencing students' choices in this fashion, we would in turn put pressure on colleges and universities to strengthen their educational programs. Since this knowledge still eludes our grasp, however, asking universities to disclose more information is a bit like trying to play Hamlet without the Dane: the exercise will have its valuable moments, but the total experience will leave much to be desired. Better information may induce institutions to work a bit harder to enlarge their libraries, expand their facilities, or increase the number of Ph.D.'s on their faculties, but all of these measurable criteria bear only an indirect and tenuous relation to the quality of learning.

Finally, government agencies and foundations could do much more to fund efforts to improve the process of education. Such assistance might take many forms: helping to start centers to improve teaching through videotaping and other useful techniques, backing promising computer programs and applications, supporting serious efforts to teach new professional skills. Funding agencies might also support research on the effectiveness of teaching and learning. In time, such assistance could give professors the feedback that will encourage them to continue trying new methods of instruction while offering faculties the chance to improve the quality of education through an informed process of trial and error. In these various ways, outside support could do much to maintain a healthy balance between teaching and research and to emphasize the importance of learning as a subject worthy of systematic study and experimentation.

In the end, though all of the measures just described may help to strengthen the environment for effective learning, their cumulative weight will still fall short of guaranteeing that each college and university performs at close to its potential. There is no ideal system now, nor will there be one in the future that can force every institution to work as conscientiously as it should to improve its educational programs. The impetus must come from within. Boards of trustees must look for presidents who share a concern for the quality of education and then provide them with an administrative structure that will allow them to exercise academic leadership. Presidents must take the initiative to articulate educational goals while providing the encouragement and material support to persuade faculty members to join in making needed improvements. Above all, faculties must regard the process of learning as an absorbing subject in its own right, worthy of continuing discussion, reflection, and experimentation.

No one can be certain how successfully our institutions will respond to this challenge. As we weigh the prospects, however, we should take heart from the fact that, on the whole, our colleges and universities are already performing quite well—in some respects, remarkably so. At one and the same time, higher education in the United States is unequaled in the world and yet falls noticeably short of the ideal. The qualities of autonomy and competition that have been instrumental in lifting our universities to their current, enviable state are still not sufficient to achieve the highest quality of teaching and learning. In sum, American universities do not face a crisis or a utopia, only a chance to make the most of a legacy of promising experiments and new opportunities to move perceptibly forward in a difficult, often inscrutable, but critical human enterprise. The effort we invest in this endeavor will ultimately depend on the faith we put in the value of education. Progress will not be rapid under the best of circumstances; its fruits may not be evident for a long time to come. Still, the stakes for our society in improving the quality of education make it imperative to try. Rather than hesitate, therefore, universities should do their best to capitalize on the opportunities before them, emboldened by the story President Kennedy used to tell about the French Marshal Louis Lyautey. When the Marshal announced that he wished to plant a tree, his gardener responded that the tree would not reach full growth for more than a hundred years. "In that case," Lyautey replied, "we have no time to lose. We must start to plant this afternoon."

Index